PARTY CAKES

for kids

This edition first published in Canada in 2006 by Whitecap Books,
351 Lynn Ave., North Vancouver, British Columbia, Canada, V7J 2C4.
www.whitecap.ca

First published by Murdoch Books Pty Limited in 2006.
www.murdochbooks.com.au

Chief Executive: Juliet Rogers
Publisher: Kay Scarlett

Photographers: Ian Hofstetter (openers and cover), Oliver Ford
Stylists: Jane Collins (openers and cover), Carolyn Fienberg
Designer: Susanne Geppert
Project manager: Jacqueline Blanchard
Editor: Zoë Harpham and Jacqueline Blanchard
Food editors: Melita Smilovic, Kathy Knudsen, Michelle Lawton, Denise Munro, Tracey Port, Wendy Quisumbing, Tracy Rutherford, Lovoni Welch
Introductory text: Tracey Port
Food preparation: Alison Adams, Renee Aitken, Justin Finlay, Wendy Quisumbing, Tracy Rutherford, Lovoni Welch
Cake decoration: Justin Finlay, Kim Passenger, Tracy Rutherford
Templates: Steve Pollitt
Production: Maiya Levitch

ISBN 1 55285 825 1
ISBN 978 1 55285 825 7

Printed by Midas Printing (Asia) Ltd.
PRINTED IN CHINA.
©Murdoch Books Pty Limited 2006.

IMPORTANT: Those who might be at risk from the effects of salmonella poisoning (the elderly, pregnant women, young children and those suffering from immune deficiency diseases) should consult their doctor with any concerns about eating raw eggs.

CONVERSION GUIDE: You may find cooking times vary depending on the oven you are using. For fan-forced ovens, as a general rule, set the oven temperature to 20°C (70°F) lower than indicated in the recipe. We have used 20 ml (4 teaspoon) tablespoon measures. If you are using a 15 ml (3 teaspoon) tablespoon, for most recipes the difference will not be noticeable. However, for recipes using baking powder, gelatine, bicarbonate of soda (baking soda) or small amounts of cornflour (cornstarch), add an extra teaspoon for each tablespoon specified.

PARTY CAKES
for kids

whitecap

contents

before you start

A birthday cake is the centrepiece of every birthday party, but it should be simple enough that there is plenty of time and energy left for planning the party. Our aim has been to create cakes that spark your child's imagination and are within easy reach of busy parents. All the cakes can be made with packet cake mix and easy-to-find decorations. As for the techniques, they are simple enough for the home cook to do with relative ease. Read below for all the basics and tips of the trade that will help turn cake decorating into a trouble-free (and fun) experience!

The best (and most logical) place to begin is the cake recipe itself as it covers everything you need to know about the cake. It is a good idea to familiarize yourself with the recipe at least a few days before the birthday party to make sure that you have everything.

cake tins

It might seem obvious, but it is essential that you use the right tin(s) for each cake. All the cooking times, quantities and templates have been based on the tins specified in the recipes. You will find the necessary tin(s) listed in the equipment list for each cake. To find out the size of a tin, turn it upside down and measure across the middle of the base with a ruler. The tins used in this book are fairly standard ones and are available at large supermarkets, department stores and some hardware stores. If you do have trouble, try a kitchenware shop.

caring for your tins Most standard tins are made from aluminium, while the more unusual shaped tins are made from specially treated tin. If yours are made from tin, dry them completely before storing or they will rust.

greasing and lining tins To prevent any cake sticking to the tins when cooking, grease and line them before baking. First, cut baking paper to the shape of the base of the tins. Next, grease your tins with either melted butter or oil — apply it evenly but not too thickly with a pastry brush, taking care to coat the corners. Vegetable oil sprays may also be used; apply in a well-ventilated area away from any heat source. After greasing, line your tin with the piece of baking paper you have cut. If you don't have paper, sprinkle the greased tin with plain flour, turning the tin to coat the base and sides evenly. Shake off any excess flour by gently tapping the upturned tin.

the basic cakes

All the cakes in this book have been made using 340 g (11¾ oz) packets of butter cake mix. But you need not feel limited to butter cake — the plainer cake mixes, such as chocolate, will work just as well. If you want to make your own, see the recipes on page 10.

baking the cakes Once the cake mix is made, pour it into the tin, then smooth the surface and bake in the centre of the oven. If you have a fan-forced oven, reduce your oven temperature by 10–20°C (50–70°F) as they are hotter than conventional ovens.

cooking times Many of the party cakes use more than one packet cake, so we have based the cooking times on the assumption that both cakes will be cooked at the same time, unless otherwise stated in the recipe. Where possible, bake the cakes on the same shelf of the oven without the tins touching. If your oven isn't large enough to fit both on one shelf, cook them on separate shelves on either side of the oven. Of course, you can also cook them one at a time; if so, see the packet for the cooking time. Because there are so many variables, we give a span in the cooking times — you should check the cakes at the earlier time.

when is the cake cooked? A cake is cooked when it begins to shrink away from the sides of the tin. A skewer inserted into the centre of the cake should come out clean — if not, return the cake to the oven until it is cooked through. Do not test a cake through a crack as this may give an incorrect result.

A cake is quite fragile when removed from the oven so leave it in the tin for 5–10 minutes to firm up before turning onto a wire rack to cool completely. If the cake seems to be stuck, gently run a flat-bladed knife around the sides to release the cake. Gently peel away the lining paper immediately.

ahead of time

Making the base cakes ahead of time not only means less for you to do on the party day itself, but it also minimizes crumbs sticking to the icing (frosting) when you are decorating. Transfer the cooled cake to an airtight container and store in a cool place for up to 3 days or freeze for up to 3 months. If freezing, thaw for 2 hours before decorating. If you do make the cake on the day, cool it completely before you decorate it.

cake boards

You will need a cake plate or cake board to support the cake, not only when you are serving, but also while you are decorating, because if you move the cake once it is decorated you risk cracking the icing (frosting) or breaking the cake. Cake boards can be made from masonite or a similar strong board which has been wrapped in paper or contact. A non-absorbent paper is the best as the oils from the cake and icing (frosting) can seep into absorbent paper and leave an unattractive mark.

covering cake boards To cover a square or rectangular board, cut a piece of paper 5 cm (2 inches) larger than the board. Cut into the corners, then fold the paper over the edge of the cake board and tape to the underside of the board. To cover a round cake board, place the board on an upside down piece of paper. Draw around the board, then draw an outline 5 cm (2 inches) larger than the board. Cut out the paper following the larger outline. Make cuts to the smaller outline about 1 cm (½ inch) apart. Replace the board in the centre of the paper and fold the cut edge over. Stick to the bottom of the board with tape.

which way up?

Once the cake is cool and the cake board is covered, the next step is to prepare the cake. In most cases, it is best to have the top side of the cake facing up as the baked smooth surface makes it easier to see any markings you might have to make.

However, sometimes you will need to level cakes, either to remove a dome to give a flat surface, or to make two adjoining cakes the same level. If so, invert the cakes as the uncut surface is easier to ice (frost). Cakes should be levelled with a serrated knife — the teeth on serrated knives give a sharper cutting action than most flat-bladed knives.

All of our party cakes have been double-tested by our team of home economists. When we test our cakes, we rate them for ease of preparation. The following cookery ratings are on the cakes in this book, making them easy to use and understand.

 A single cupcake indicates a cake that is simple and relatively quick to make — perfect for beginners.

 Two cupcakes indicate the need for just a little more care and some more time.

 Three cupcakes indicate party cakes that require a greater investment in time, care and patience — but the results are well worth it.

joining cakes

If your party cake uses more than one base cake, you will need to join them. Place the undecorated, cooled and trimmed cakes on the cake board and use icing (frosting) or warm jam to join them. If you have to join two cakes that sit on top of one another, never use toothpicks: they can get lost and may accidentally be served to a child. Use skewers because they are more obvious and easy to remove before serving.

how to use the templates

Some of the cakes have a template to help you cut and decorate the cake. The templates are very easy to use, especially if you have access to a photocopier. Photocopy your chosen template from the back of the book and enlarge it by the percentage given to achieve the desired size. If the enlarged image is greater than your copy paper, you may need to increase the size over several areas of the image, then piece the paper together using sticky (adhesive) tape. It's a good idea to do more than one copy just in case you make any mistakes.

If you don't have access to a photocopier, draw a graph with squares the size indicated under the template, then transfer the image onto the larger graph.

Once you have your template copied, cut it out, sit it on the cake and secure at a few anchor points with toothpicks to prevent the template moving when cutting. Some of the templates have features that need to be transferred onto the cake. To do this, pierce through the paper with a skewer or toothpick.

making the icing (frosting)

We have used three different types of icing to decorate our cakes: buttercream, meringue frosting and white chocolate ganache. See page 11 for the recipes.

food colourings

In most cases, the icing (frosting) will need to be coloured — you can use powdered, liquid and paste food colourings, which can be purchased from cake-decorating suppliers, supermarkets, large craft and fabric stores and some health food stores. For darker or bolder colours such as black, navy or red it is best to use powders or pastes as they give a much truer colour than liquid.

powders and pastes   Powdered food colourings can be used in two ways. The first way is to dissolve the powder in a small amount of water before stirring into the icing (frosting) — this ensures even and quick distribution through the icing (frosting). Alternatively, they can be added directly to the icing (frosting); however, mixing will take a little longer to prevent the icing (frosting) becoming streaked with small specks of concentrated colour. Pastes are easily mixed straight into icing (frosting) a little at a time. Use the end of a small spoon or the tip of a knife to add pastes and powders. Never dip a moist or dirty skewer or knife into colours as this can make them go off.

liquids   Liquids are generally the least concentrated but most readily available of the food colourings. Use a clean dropper or the tip of a clean skewer dipped in liquid colours and add gradually to achieve the desired colour. Don't be afraid to mix colours to achieve the colour you want. A colour wheel or art book can help you to know what colours to mix, otherwise experiment in a small bowl before adding to the icing (frosting).

how to ice (frost) the cake

Once the icing is tinted, it needs to be spread onto the cake. In most cases it is best to use a flat-bladed knife or palette knife. However, you may find it easier to first pipe the icing onto the smaller areas like the eyes or when a lot of different coloured icings are used. After you have piped on the icing, spread it smooth with a palette knife. For really smooth icing, heat your knife in hot water and wipe it dry before dipping in the icing and smoothing. Repeat this process between each stroke.

Palette knives can be purchased at speciality kitchen shops and come in various lengths and widths. It is good to have a small and a large palette knife for icing different areas, but a good multi-purpose one has a 10 cm (4 inch) blade.

decoration

Once the cake is iced (frosted), some cakes are nearly completed, but others need the decorative touches like lollies (candy) and toys. All of these should be readily available from supermarkets or you can make substitutes and improvise easily.

lollies (candy) Lollies are great for easy decorating as they come in a huge range of colours, shapes and sizes and can be easily stuck on the cake with a dab of leftover icing (frosting). We have taken care to use lollies and decorations that are readily available. Many supermarkets carry 'pick and choose' lolly selections where you can buy just a few of one type of lolly instead of a whole packet. Otherwise use the leftovers for childrens' lolly bags. Speciality shops often sell a wide variety of more unusual and imported lollies.

The lollies we have used can usually be substituted with a similar shaped lolly or, if you are feeling creative, with others that you prefer. Lollies to be trimmed or cut, such as liquorice straps, marshmallows or jellybeans, may be cut with a sharp knife or scissors. To cut sticky lollies such as marshmallows, dip the scissors or knife in icing (confectioners') sugar or cornflour (cornstarch) before cutting so that the scissors don't stick together.

For safety reasons it is best to avoid hard lollies and nuts on cakes for children under 3 years of age. Use soft lollies or coloured sprinkles (sugar strands) instead to avoid choking.

other decorations Non-edible decorations have been bought from toy shops, supermarkets, craft shops, speciality shops and department stores. These are not always absolutely necessary and can be substituted for similar items.

detailing

To mark the outline and highlights on cakes, we have used food gels, melted chocolate, piped icing (frosting) and thin strips of liquorice.

gels Edible gels come in a variety of different colours and are very easy to use as they can be squeezed straight from the tube.

melted chocolate To melt chocolate, chop the chocolate (or the chocolate melts or buttons) and place it in a heatproof bowl. Bring a saucepan of water to the boil and remove from the heat. Sit the bowl over the pan, making sure the base of the bowl is not touching the water. Stir occasionally, until the chocolate has melted. Alternatively, put the chocolate in a microwave-safe bowl and microwave on High in 30-second bursts, testing each time until melted.

piped icing (frosting) Sometimes we use leftover icing to add the edging around cakes. For this, you need a piping bag. To make a piping bag, cut a 30 cm (12 inch) square of baking paper in half diagonally. Twist the triangle into a cone shape (the centre of the long side should end up being the tip of the piping bag). Fold the paper over at the other end to hold its shape. Fill the cone half to two-thirds full with icing or melted chocolate, then seal by folding over the edges to keep the filling contained. Alternatively, you can use a small plastic bag: spoon the icing or chocolate into the corner of a small plastic bag, twist the top of the bag to secure, then snip the corner tip off the bag to pipe.

When piping, apply even pressure and make smooth movements to prevent the icing clumping and breaking the line. Hold the piping bag at a 45-degree angle when piping and squeeze gently from the top.

serving sizes

Generally a 3–4 cm (1 1/4 – 1 1/2 inch) square piece of cake per child is sufficient for a children's party.

storing

To store a decorated cake, either lift the cake on its cake board into a container or, if the cake is too large, upturn a large box over the cake. Cakes can be stored for 2–3 days in a cool dry place when iced (frosted) with buttercream. Meringue frosting should be stored at room temperature and eaten within 24 hours. Chocolate ganache icings (frostings) are best in a cool dry place unless it is really hot when refrigeration will be necessary; however, it can make the chocolate sweat and cause discolouring.

transporting cakes

If you have to move your party cake once it is decorated, place it in a clean covered box that is the size of the cake board. If your box is too big, roll pieces of sticky (adhesive) tape and put on the bottom of the cake board or straight into the bottom of the box to prevent the cake from sliding. Press firmly into the box to secure the cake. Put the boxed cake on a non-slip mat or sheet on a flat surface — on the floor or in the boot of the car, not on the seat. Drive very carefully and take some leftover icing, a spare piping bag and a palette knife in case of touch-ups.

basic cake recipes

We used 340 g (11 3/4 oz) packets of butter cake mix to make our cakes. If you would prefer to make your own, the basic cake recipes here are equivalent to one packet cake. Once the cake is cooled, wrap it in plastic wrap or place in an airtight container: either store in a cool, dry place for up to 3 days or freeze for up to 3 months. If you are freezing your cake, thaw it for 2 hours before you start decorating.

butter cake

Preparation time: 25 minutes
Total cooking time: 45 minutes

150 g (5 1/2 oz) butter, softened
115 g (4 oz / 1/2 cup) caster (superfine)
   sugar
2 eggs, lightly beaten
1 1/2 teaspoons natural vanilla extract
185 g (6 1/2 oz / 1 1/2 cups) self-raising
   flour
80 ml (2 1/2 fl oz / 1/3 cup) milk

1 Preheat the oven to 180°C (350°F/Gas 4). Lightly grease a deep 20 cm (8 inch) round cake tin and line the base with baking paper.

2 Beat the butter and sugar with electric beaters until light and creamy. Add the eggs one at a time, beating well after each addition. Add the natural vanilla extract and beat until combined.

3 Using a large metal spoon, fold in the sifted flour alternately with the milk until smooth. Spoon the mixture into the tin and smooth the surface. Bake for 45 minutes, or until a skewer comes out clean when inserted into the centre of the cake.

4 Leave the cake in the tin for at least 5 minutes before turning out onto a wire rack to cool completely.

chocolate cake

Preparation time: 25 minutes
Total cooking time: 45 minutes

150 g (5 1/2 oz) butter, softened
175 g (6 oz / 3/4 cup) caster (superfine)
   sugar
2 eggs, lightly beaten
1 teaspoon natural vanilla extract
215 g (7 1/2 oz / 1 3/4 cups) self-raising
   flour
60 g (2 1/4 oz / 1/2 cup) unsweetened
   cocoa powder
185 ml (6 fl oz / 3/4 cup) milk

1 Preheat the oven to 180°C (350°F/Gas 4). Lightly grease a deep 20 cm (8 inch) round cake tin and line the base with baking paper.

2 Beat the butter and sugar in a large bowl with electric beaters until light and creamy. Add the eggs gradually, beating thoroughly after each addition. Add the natural vanilla extract and beat well.

3 Using a metal spoon, fold in the sifted flour and cocoa powder alternately with the milk. Stir until just smooth.

4 Spoon the mixture into the tin and smooth the surface. Bake for 45 minutes, or until a skewer comes out clean when inserted in the centre. Leave the cake to cool in the tin for at least 5 minutes before turning out on a wire rack to cool completely.

the icing on the cake

Each of these icings (frostings) makes one quantity. If your cake needs more than one quantity of icing (frosting), increase the ingredients proportionally. Each icing (frosting) will cover a 20 cm (8 inch) square or round cake.

buttercream

1. Beat the butter in a small bowl with electric beaters until pale and fluffy.

2. Continue beating and gradually add the natural vanilla extract and half the sifted icing sugar.

3. Gradually add the milk and the remaining sugar and beat until smooth.

   VARIATION: To make chocolate buttercream, mix 2 tablespoons of sifted unsweetened cocoa powder into the mixture.

125 g (4½ oz) good-quality unsalted butter, at room temperature
1 teaspoon natural vanilla extract
185 g (6½ oz/1½ cups) icing (confectioner's) sugar
2 tablespoons milk, at room temperature

meringue frosting

1. Stir the sugar and 80 ml (2½ fl oz/⅓ cup) water in a saucepan over low heat until the sugar has dissolved — do not allow to boil. Brush any sugar grains from the side of the pan with a pastry brush dipped in water. Increase the heat and boil without stirring for 3–5 minutes or until it reaches soft ball stage (115°C/225°F on a sugar thermometer). Test by dropping a teaspoon of syrup into cold water — it will form a soft sticky ball.

2. While the syrup is boiling, beat the egg whites with electric beaters in a small bowl until firm peaks form. When the syrup bubbles subside, gradually pour the syrup in a thin stream onto the whites, beating (the beaters should be on medium speed). It will thicken and form stiff peaks.

230 g (8 oz/1 cup) caster (superfine) sugar
2 egg whites

white chocolate ganache

1. Put all the ingredients in a saucepan and stir over low heat until melted and smooth.

2. Transfer the mixture to a small bowl, cover the surface with plastic wrap and leave to cool completely. Do not refrigerate or it will go hard.

3. When cooled, beat with electric beaters for 8–10 minutes, or until thick, pale and creamy.

150 g (5½ oz/1 cup) white chocolate melts (buttons)
150 g (5½ oz/1 cup) white chocolate, chopped
125 ml (4 fl oz/½ cup) cream (whipping)
250 g (9 oz) unsalted butter, chopped

enchanted
folk

enchanted village

CAKE AND EQUIPMENT

giant muffin tin

½ packet cake mix

four 15 cm (6 inch) jam (jelly) rolls

three 5 cm (2 inch) jam rollettes (mini jelly rolls)

35 x 35 cm (14 x 14 inch) cake board

DECORATION

2½ quantities buttercream from page 11

food colourings: rose and violet

180 g (6½ oz/1½ cups) pink heart lollies (candies)

150 g (5½ oz/1 cup) white mints

250 g (9 oz/or about 25) pink musk sticks (candy sticks)

assorted marshmallows

assorted pastel coloured lollies (candies)

1   Preheat the oven to 180°C (350°F/Gas 4). Lightly grease three holes of a giant muffin tin. Fill the holes three-quarters full with the cake mix, then bake for 20–25 minutes, or until cooked through. Cool in the tins, then loosen each muffin and turn out onto a wire rack to cool completely.

2   Cut one of the large jam rolls in half. Cut one third off another of the large jam rolls to create a large and a small roll. Trim the ends off all the rolls and rollettes so that they are level.

3   Cut the dome tops off the muffins, then turn over and trim the bottom of each muffin to resemble pointed roof tops.

4   Divide the buttercream equally between two bowls. Add a little rose colouring to one half and a little violet to the other half.

5   Stand lengths of the rolls on the cake board to form the buildings of the village, with the tallest rolls at the back. Once you are happy with the shape of your village, affix either a rollette or muffin for the roof of each building.

6   Ice the buildings and roofs with the two colours so that three are pink and three are purple and affix to the cake board with a little extra buttercream. Finish the roofs by decorating one with heart lollies, one with halved mints, one with thinly sliced musk sticks and the others with marshmallows — you may need a little extra buttercream to fasten the roof 'tiles' in place.

7   To give the impression of brickwork, use a skewer to draw bricks into the walls of some of the buildings. Decorate the buildings with windows, doors, turrets and other features made out of lollies.

8   For the final touch, spread buttercream to make a couple of pathways leading away from the village and sprinkle with assorted lollies.

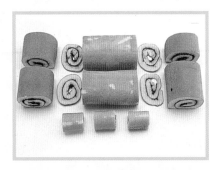

Trim the ends of the rolls; cut one in half and cut a third off another roll.

Cut the bottom of the muffins into the shape of a roof top.

Top the tower bodies with muffin roof tops or jam rollettes.

cuddly teddy bear

1   Preheat the oven to 180°C (350°F/Gas 4). Grease the cake tins and pudding basin and line the bases with baking paper. Divide the cake mix evenly among the three tins and bake for 35–40 minutes, or until a skewer inserted into the centre of the cakes comes out clean. Most ovens will fit all three cakes — make sure they are not touching; if they are, cook separately. Cool in the tins for 5 minutes, then turn out onto a wire rack to cool completely.

2   Level the two round cakes, if necessary. Sit one of the cakes on the cake board and spread the top with buttercream. Sandwich the two cakes together. Trim a diagonal strip off the top and bottom edges of the cake sandwich to form a fat body. Sit the pudding-shaped cake on the body, with the flat side of the pudding on top. Push two skewers through the head and body to firmly secure them together. Trim any protruding skewer. Trim a diagonal slice around the bottom edge of the pudding to create a neck.

3   Cut a diagonal slice off the flat end of four rollettes and attach them to the body with skewers — two for the arms and two for the legs. Cut a 1.5 cm (³/₄ inch) slice off the remaining rollette and stick it onto the centre of the face with a skewer — this is the snout. Make two slits on the top of the head where the ears should go, then push a biscuit into each slit.

4   Tint ¹/₃ cup of the buttercream white. Add the cocoa to the remainder and beat well. Thickly spread the chocolate buttercream over the body, arms and legs (reserve a tablespoon for piping). Ice (frost) the tummy, snout and ears white. Rough up the buttercream with a palette knife so that it looks like fur.

5   To make the eyes, cut a marshmallow in half and stick a brown lolly on each half with a dab of buttercream. Put the eyes in place. Use thin strips of liquorice for the lips, a triangular piece for the nose and a red jellybean for the mouth. Use a brown sugar-coated lolly for a belly button. Using a piping bag filled with the reserved chocolate buttercream, pipe four small dots and one large dot on each chocolate melt for the paws, then press them gently in place.

CAKE AND EQUIPMENT

two 18 cm (7 inch) round cake tins
1 litre (35 fl oz/4 cups) metal pudding basin (mould)
2 packets cake mix
30 cm (12 inch) round cake board
five 5 cm (2 inch) jam rollettes
skewers
ruler

DECORATION

1¹/₂ quantities buttercream from page 11
2 round chocolate biscuits (cookies)
30 g (1 oz/¹/₄ cup) unsweetened cocoa powder, sifted
1 white marshmallow
3 brown sugar-coated chocolate lollies (candies)
liquorice pieces
1 red jellybean
4 white chocolate melts (buttons)

Trim a diagonal slice around the top and bottom of the cakes to create a body.

Cut a diagonal slice all around the bottom of the head to create a neck.

Secure the rollettes to the body with skewers.

marvin the martian

CAKE AND EQUIPMENT
20 cm (8 inch) round cake tin
1 packet cake mix
30 cm (12 inch) round cake board
copy of template from page 126
toothpicks or skewers

DECORATION
1 quantity buttercream from page 11
green food colouring
hundreds and thousands (nonpareils)
sugar-coated chocolate lollies (candies)
blue and red cake decorating gels
1 marshmallow
mini jubes (gumdrops/fruit pastilles)
2 red lollipops

1 Preheat the oven to 180°C (350°F/Gas 4). Grease the cake tin and line the base with baking paper. Spoon the mixture into the tin and bake for 35–40 minutes, or until a skewer inserted into the centre of the cake comes out clean. Let the cake cool in the tin for 5 minutes before turning out onto a wire rack to cool completely.

2 Stick the crescent template onto the edge of the cake and secure it with skewers — if you think you will need help cutting out the neck, mark the neck marks onto the cake with a skewer or a toothpick. Cut out the crescent with a sharp knife. Remove the template and toothpicks, then cut the neck piece out from the middle of the crescent — keep the two side pieces for the ears.

3 Tint the buttercream bright green. Place the large piece of cake on the cake board and cover it with buttercream. Put the neck piece into position in the middle of the least curved side of the cake. Ice (frost) the neck with the buttercream.

4 Trim the domed top of the two ears so that they are level, then cover them with buttercream. Dip the ears into a saucer filled with hundreds and thousands to coat them all over. Stick the ears into position on either side of the head and attach a yellow sugar-coated chocolate lolly to the tip of each with a little bit of buttercream.

5 Mark three ovals for the eyes onto the face with a toothpick or skewer, then fill the outlines with red gel. Cut the marshmallow into thirds and place one third on each oval. Top each one with a blue sugar-coated chocolate lolly, securing with a little gel.

6 Put two red sugar-coated chocolate lollies into place for the nostrils, five mini jubes across the forehead, and three across the neck. Pipe a zigzag mouth with the blue gel and insert two lollipops into the top of the head for antennae.

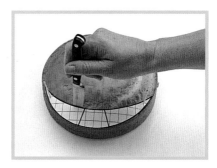

Stick the crescent template on the edge of the cake and cut the cake to shape.

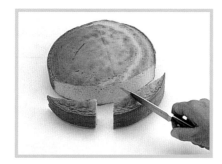

Cut out the neck piece from the cake crescent.

Stick the neck piece into position in the middle of the flatter side of the head.

Roll the ears in the hundreds and thousands until well covered.

fairy princess

1   Remove the ice cream from the freezer for 15 minutes to soften a little. While you are waiting, make some space in the freezer wide enough to fit a 25 cm (10 inch) cake plate and tall enough to fit the pudding basin and the doll. Line the pudding basin with plastic wrap with the ends overhanging the side. Transfer the ice cream to a large bowl and 'mash' with a potato masher to help soften the ice cream, then spoon it into the lined pudding basin, smoothing the surface evenly. Cover the top of the ice cream with the overhanging plastic wrap and freeze for at least 4 hours, or until firm.

2   Take the tin out of the freezer and, working quickly, dip the base into warm water. Pull back the plastic wrap, put the cake plate over the tin and invert the ice cream onto the plate, then remove the basin and plastic wrap. Return the ice cream mound on its plate to the freezer for 1 hour, or until set.

3   Remove the ice cream from the freezer and, working quickly, use a teaspoon to scoop out enough ice cream from the top of the mound to sit the doll in up to her waist. Spoon back the ice cream around the doll to cement her into place. Tie the doll's hair back or cover it with plastic wrap to prevent her hair falling into the ice cream while decorating. Return to the freezer for 1 hour.

4   Put the cream and caster sugar in a bowl and begin whisking. Add a few drops of colouring at a time and whisk until firm peaks form. Remove the princess from the freezer. Using a spatula, cover the ice cream skirt with the whipped cream and shape into soft waves with a palette knife. Decorate the skirt with the silver dragées and sugared flowers, then return to the freezer for 1 hour, or until the cream is set.

5   Remove from the freezer. Wrap the dark ribbon around the body of the doll and seal at the back with sticky tape. Wrap the sheer piece of ribbon over the dark bodice and tie a big bow at the back to resemble wings. Groom the princess's hair and crown her with the tiara. Return to the freezer until ready to serve.

CAKE AND EQUIPMENT
4 litres (140 fl oz/16 cups) ice cream
2 litre (70 fl oz/8 cups) pudding basin (mould)
25 cm (10 inch) cake plate or board
small plastic doll with legs removed
sticky (adhesive) tape

DECORATION
600 ml (21 fl oz/2½ cups) thick (double/heavy) cream
1 tablespoon caster (superfine) sugar
yellow food colouring
silver dragées or cachous
yellow and pink sugared flowers (see Note)
20 cm (8 inch) length of solid pink ribbon
1 metre (3 ft) length of sheer ribbon
1 tiara

NOTE
We bought sugared flowers from a specialist cake decorating shop. You can also use material ones available from fabric shops, but remember to remove them before serving.

Spoon the softened ice cream into the lined pudding basin.

Invert the frozen ice cream mound onto a cake plate.

Spoon ice cream back into the hole around the doll to cement her in place.

desmond the dinosaur

CAKE AND EQUIPMENT
23 cm (9 inch) square cake tin
20 x 30 cm (8 x 12 inch) rectangular
   cake tin
3 packets cake mix
32 x 60 cm (13 x 24 inch) cake board
copy of template from page 127
toothpicks or skewers

DECORATION
2 quantities buttercream from page 11
food colourings: violet and black
   (we used powder)
2 mini white marshmallows
small and large green sugar-coated
   chocolate lollies (candies)

1 Preheat the oven to 180°C (350°F/Gas 4). Grease the cake tins and line the bases with baking paper. Divide the mixture evenly between the tins and bake the square cake for 45–50 minutes, then the rectangular cake for 25–30 minutes, or until a skewer inserted into the centre of the cakes comes out clean. Let the cakes cool in the tins for 5 minutes before turning out onto a wire rack to cool completely.

2 Put about ¾ cup of the buttercream in a small bowl and tint it black. Tint the larger portion of the buttercream violet.

3 Arrange the cakes on the board as shown and secure with some buttercream. Position the template onto the cakes and secure with toothpicks. Cut the cakes to shape, then remove the template and toothpicks.

4 Spread violet buttercream over the whole cake, including the sides. Copying the template or picture, use a skewer or toothpick to draw the outlines and all the features onto the dinosaur — if you make a mistake, you can smooth it over and start again. Once you have the features marked out, contour the buttercream on the neck and legs with a palette knife, being careful not to erase your skewer marks. Pipe the outlines of the dinosaur with black buttercream, using your skewer marks as a guide.

5 Flatten the marshmallows slightly and put them into position for the eyes. Pipe a small dot on each marshmallow for the pupils. Arrange the lollies randomly over the cake as shown.

Arrange the cakes on a cake board and stick together with a little buttercream.

Stick the template onto the cake with the toothpicks.

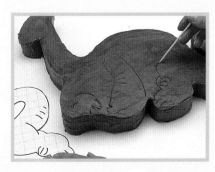

Use a skewer or toothpick to trace the outline of the dinosaur's features.

Go over your skewer marks with the piping bag filled with black buttercream.

splash! mermaid

1. Preheat the oven to 180°C (350°F/Gas 4). Grease the cake tins and line the bases with baking paper. Divide the cake mix evenly between the tins and bake (they should fit on the same shelf) for 25–30 minutes, or until a skewer inserted into the centre of the cakes comes out clean. Let the cakes cool in the tins for 5 minutes before turning out onto a wire rack to cool completely.

2. Put the cakes on the cake board in a backwards L shape, joining the edges with a little buttercream — level them so they are an even height. Position the template onto the cake and secure with toothpicks. Mark the bodice onto the cake by piercing through the paper with a skewer or toothpick. Using a small sharp knife, cut the cake to shape. Remove the template and toothpicks.

3. Put one half of the buttercream in one bowl, then divide the remaining buttercream in half again and put each portion in a separate bowl. Tint the largest portion pale green, one portion blue and the other portion pale peach. Ice (frost) the tail green, the bodice blue and the head, neck, chest and arms peach. Use a palette knife to give the buttercream on the tail a swirled texture.

4. Lightly sprinkle green sugar crystals over the tail. Decorate the bodice with dragées (we used silver, but you may prefer to decorate with a variety of colours), then make a necklace out of different coloured dragées.

5. To make the hair, flatten the fruit bars with a rolling pin, then slice into thin strips. Arrange the hair around the face and cascading over the shoulders. Pipe the mermaid's features onto her face with cake decorating gels: red for the mouth, black for the eyes and nose and blue for the pupils.

CAKE AND EQUIPMENT
two 20 x 30 cm (8 x 12 inch)
   rectangular cake tins
3 packets cake mix
30 x 50 cm (12 x 20 inch) cake board
copy of template from page 128
toothpicks or skewers

DECORATION
2 quantities buttercream from page 11
food colourings: blue, green and peach
green sugar crystals (see Note)
assorted dragées or cachous
4 apricot fruit bars
cake decorating gels: red, black and blue

NOTE
We bought ready-made coloured sugar crystals, but you can make your own by placing sugar in a plastic bag and adding a drop or two of liquid food colouring. Close the bag and shake the bag until the colour disperses through the sugar.

Form the cakes into a backwards L shape and stick the template in place.

Once you have iced (frosted) the mermaid, create swirls on the tail and bodice.

Use a sharp knife to cut very thin strips from the flattened fruit bars.

cranky witch

CAKE AND EQUIPMENT
two 1.5 litre (52 fl oz/6 cups) round-
    based pudding basins (moulds)
2 packets cake mix
30 cm (12 inch) square cake board
2 skewers
ruler

HAT
copy of template from page 129
cardboard and stickers

DECORATION
2 quantities buttercream from page 11
food colourings: blue, peach and black
    (we used powder for black)
1 ice cream cone
1 musk stick (candy stick)
2 x 1 metre (3 ft) long liquorice straps
2 chocolate jewels (chocolate
    nonpareils/rainbow drops)
2 brown sugar-coated chocolate lollies
    (candies)
black cake decorating gel

1 Preheat the oven to 180°C (350°F/Gas 4). Grease the pudding basins and line the bases with baking paper. Divide the cake mix evenly between the basins and bake for 40–45 minutes, or until a skewer comes out clean. Cool in the tins for 5 minutes before turning out onto a wire rack to cool completely.

2 Sit the cakes on top of each other and secure with two skewers. Trim the sides of the top cake to form the round head. Shave down the sides of the base cake at a 45-degree angle to form a body. Cut two triangles from the off-cuts to create two arms.

3 Put three-quarters of the buttercream in a bowl and tint it blue. Put 1/2 cup of the remaining buttercream in another bowl and tint it pale peach. Tint the remaining buttercream black.

4 Ice (frost) the body blue and spread the peach buttercream over the face area. Stick the tip of the ice cream cone onto the middle of the face and ice (frost) it peach. Spread black buttercream over the back and top of the head.

5 Attach the arms to the body (you might need a skewer) and cover the sleeve with blue buttercream, but ice (frost) the hands peach. Attach the musk stick between the arms as a broom handle.

6 Cut six 14 cm (5 1/2 inch) lengths and three 5 cm (2 inch) lengths of liquorice. Cut into thin strips, but don't cut all the way through the strap (see picture).

7 Use the long lengths of liquorice for the hair and use two of the shorter lengths as a fringe. Attach the final piece of liquorice to the dress at the end of the musk stick for the broom head.

8 To make the spider, put two spots of icing (frosting) on the cake board and stick on two jewels and add legs of thin strips of liquorice.

9 Use two brown lollies for the eyes. Pipe the facial features with black gel so that the witch looks cranky. Add an extra two drops of blue food colouring to the remaining blue buttercream, transfer to a piping bag and pipe stripes at the front of the dress to make gathers.

10 Use the template to cut the cardboard into pieces for the hat. Roll the triangle into a cone and secure with tape or staples. Cut a small circle about 5 cm (2 inches) in diameter out of the centre of the large circle to fit the cone into. Push the cone through the hole and secure with tape from the inside. Decorate with stickers, then put into place.

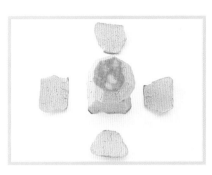

Shave off the sides of the bottom cake at a 45-degree angle.

Use one of the offcuts from the body to make two triangles for the arms.

Cut the liquorice strap into thin strips, but don't cut all the way through.

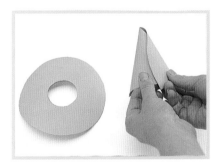

Cut out hat pieces from cardboard then join together to form the hat.

happy clown

CAKE AND EQUIPMENT
two 22 cm (8½ inch) round cake tins
3 packets cake mix
copy of template from page 130
toothpicks or skewers
28 x 48 cm (11¼ x 19 inch) cake board
ruler

DECORATION
2 quantities buttercream from page 11
food colourings: blue, yellow, green
1 metre (3 ft) long liquorice strap
2 large red gum balls (gobstoppers)
cake decorating gels: red, black
3 blue sugar-coated chocolate lollies
  (candies)
2 white marshmallows
rainbow and red fruit straps

1   Preheat the oven to 180°C (350°F/Gas 4). Grease the cake tins and line the bases with baking paper. Divide the cake mix evenly between the tins and bake for 45–50 minutes, or until a skewer inserted into the centre of the cakes comes out clean. Cool the cakes in the tins for 5 minutes before turning out onto a wire rack to cool completely.

2   Level the cakes if necessary, then turn them over. Secure the hat template to one cake and cut to shape. Pierce the paper with a skewer or toothpick to mark the lines between the stripes. Remove the template and toothpicks. Cut a 3 cm (1¼ inch) slice off the top of the other cake, leaving a straight edge. Piece the clown together on the cake board and join the pieces with buttercream.

3   Divide the buttercream in half and leave one half white, then divide the remaining mixture into thirds and tint one part blue, one part yellow and the other part green. Ice (frost) the face with the white buttercream and the hat in alternating stripes of blue and yellow. Lastly, ice (frost) the bow with the green buttercream.

4   Cut the liquorice strap into thin strips, then into the following lengths: 3.5 cm (1½ inches), 7.5 cm (3¼ inches), 12 cm (4½ inches), 16.5 cm (6½ inches) and two 19.5 cm (8 inches) for the hat; two 7 cm (2¾ inches), four 8 cm (3¼ inches), two 11 cm (4¼ inches) and two 12 cm (4½ inches) for the bow tie. Outline the hat and bow tie with these strips.

5   Stick one of the gum balls on the tip of the hat and the other one in the centre of the face. Use a skewer to mark the outline of the eyes, then go over your markings with red gel. Next, use two blue lollies stuck onto two marshmallows for the centre of the eyes. Use an extra blue lolly for the centre of the bow tie.

6   Slightly stretch out a red fruit strap and, using scissors, cut out a smiley mouth and two small round dots for the cheeks — you can either use the template or do it freehand. Press gently into place. With the black gel, fill in the outline of the mouth and add the eyelashes.

7   Just before serving, make the hair: slice the rainbow fruit straps into thin strips and twirl around a pencil to create curls. Put the hair around the face.

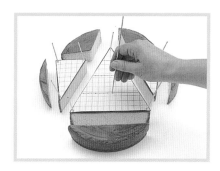

Cut out the cake pieces, then mark the stripes by piercing the cake.

Join the hat to the round cake and make a bow tie out of the small pieces.

Twist strips of fruit strap around a pencil or pen to make curls.

ferocious monster

CAKE AND EQUIPMENT

two 20 x 30 cm (8 x 12 inch)
    rectangular cake tins
3 packets cake mix
25 x 35 cm (10 x 14 inch) cake board
copy of template from page 131
toothpicks or skewers

DECORATION

2 quantities buttercream from page 11
food colourings: black and green
    (we used powder for black)
liquorice allsorts (striped liquorice
    candies)
1 metre (3 ft) long liquorice strap
red cake decorating gel or
    strawberry sauce

1   Preheat the oven to 180°C (350°F/Gas 4). Grease the cake tins and line the bases with baking paper. Divide the cake mix evenly between the tins and bake for 25–30 minutes, or until a skewer inserted into the centre of the cakes comes out clean. Let the cakes cool in the tins for 5 minutes before turning out onto a wire rack to cool completely.

2   Put the cakes on the cake board and join them along the long edges with a little buttercream. Cut out the pieces of the template and position onto the cakes as shown, securing with a few toothpicks. Cut the cakes to shape with a small sharp knife. Use a skewer or toothpick to mark out the mouth and the basic shape of the hair area by piercing through the paper onto the cake. Remove the templates and toothpicks.

3   Cut the eyes in half so that they are half their original height. Shave off one long side of the brow at a 45-degree angle to form the jutting forehead.

4   Tint three quarters of the buttercream green. Tint the remainder of the buttercream black. Ice (frost) the marked out hair and mouth sections black, reserving 2 tablespoons of the black buttercream for the outline. Ice (frost) the entire face green. Position the forehead, eyes and nose on the face, then ice (frost) them green.

5   Trim nine pieces of yellow fondant from the liquorice allsorts for the teeth. Put them in position, trimming those at the edges so that they fit the mouth.

6   Cut the liquorice strap into varying lengths and thicknesses to create stringy hair and lay over the black buttercream — don't worry about being neat. Put the reserved black buttercream in a small piping bag and pipe on all the features. Use red gel to pipe the blood dripping from the mouth.

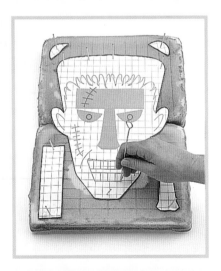
Stick the template onto the cake and mark the mouth and hair with a skewer.

Cut the eyes in half, then shave a 45-degree angle off the brow.

Once the face is iced (frosted), put the nose, eyes and forehead into position.

wonder
world

creepy-crawly caterpillar

CAKE AND EQUIPMENT

six 185 ml (6 fl oz/³/₄ cup) small pie tins
1 packet cake mix
30 x 55 cm (12 x 22 inch) cake board
copy of template from page 132
ruler

DECORATION

¹/₂ quantity white chocolate ganache
   from page 11
assorted sprinkles (sugar strands)
3 fruit rings
1 metre (3 ft) long liquorice strap

1 Preheat the oven to 190°C (375°F/Gas 5). Grease the pie tins. Line the bases with small rounds of non-stick baking paper. Divide the cake mix among the tins and bake for 15–20 minutes, or until a skewer comes out clean when inserted into the centre of the cakes. Leave in the tins for 5 minutes, then turn out onto a wire rack to cool completely.

2 Using the template, cut a small crescent from one side of five of the cakes, so they fit snugly together. These five cakes are the body pieces; the remaining round cake will be the head.

3 Spread the top of each cake with the white chocolate ganache. Cover two thirds of a cake with the template and decorate the exposed area with sprinkles. Move the template over so that more of the cake is exposed and sprinkle this crescent with different coloured sprinkles. Remove the template and sprinkle the final area with a third colour. Repeat with the other cakes, using alternating coloured sprinkles.

4 Cover the head cake all over with chocolate sprinkles. Choose two pink fruit rings which are a good round shape for the eyes, and another to cut in half for the mouth. Cut the liquorice strap into thin strips, then cut two small pieces of liquorice to fit in the eye rings. Gently scrape some of the sprinkles away from the eye and mouth areas, and press the features into place. Cut ten 4 cm (1 ½ inch) lengths of liquorice for the legs and two 5 cm (2 inch) lengths for the antennae.

5 Arrange the caterpillar on the prepared board, making the body pieces alternately slightly higher and lower, so it looks like it is wriggling. Join the pieces with a little ganache. Attach the legs and antennae by pushing into the cake; they will rest slightly on the board.

Use the template to help you make coloured stripes on the body pieces.

Stick the eyes and mouth on the face in the areas you have cleared of sprinkles.

Stick the antennae and legs into the sides of the cake and rest them on the board.

fresh as a daisy

1   Preheat the oven to 180°C (350°F/Gas 4). Grease the cake tins and line the bases with baking paper. Divide the cake mix evenly between the tins and bake for 35–40 minutes, or until a skewer inserted into the centre of the cakes comes out clean. Cool the cakes in the tins for 5 minutes before turning out onto a wire rack to cool completely.

2   Level the cakes if necessary. Position the flower template on the round cake and the leaf template on the long cake and secure with toothpicks. Cut the cakes to shape. Remove the template and toothpicks.

3   Stick one chocolate bar on top of another with a little buttercream. Repeat with the other two chocolate bars to make the stem. Sit the flower cake on the cake board, add the chocolate stem underneath the flower and put the leaves on either side of the stem.

4   Put one third of the buttercream in a bowl and tint it green, then tint the larger portion light orange. Spread the orange buttercream all over the flower, making shallow furrows in the petals with a palette knife. Put the biscuit cutter in the centre of the cake and pour orange sprinkles in the middle of it. Carefully lift off the biscuit cutter.

5   Ice the leaves with the green buttercream. Cut the spearmint leaves in half horizontally and overlap on the cake leaves. Sit the butterfly on the flower.

CAKE AND EQUIPMENT
22 cm (8½ inch) round cake tin
8 x 25 cm (3¼ x 10 inch) loaf (bar) tin
2 packets cake mix
30 x 50 cm (12 x 20 inch) cake board
copy of template from page 133
toothpicks
small round biscuit (cookie) cutter

DECORATION
4 flaked chocolate bars
2 quantities buttercream from page 11
food colourings: orange and green
orange sprinkles (sugar strands)
spearmint leaves (candied fruit leaves)
toy butterfly

Put all the cake pieces into position, using the chocolate bar as the stem.

Sit the spearmint leaves slightly overlapping each other on the cake leaves.

Once the flower has been iced (frosted), make furrows with a palette knife.

hopping rabbit

CAKE AND EQUIPMENT

two 20 x 30 cm (8 x 12 inch)
  rectangular cake tins
2 packets cake mix
copy of template from pages 134–135
40 cm (16 inch) square cake board
toothpicks

DECORATION

1 quantity white chocolate ganache
  from page 11
food colourings: orange and pink
1 spearmint leaf (candied fruit leaf)
1 pink marshmallow
35 g (1¼ oz/¼ cup) white chocolate
  melts (buttons)
1 pink sugar-coated chocolate lolly
  (candy)
5 mini mints

1   Preheat the oven to 180°C (350°F/Gas 4). Grease the cake tins and line the bases with baking paper. Divide the cake mix evenly between the tins and bake for 20–25 minutes, or until a skewer inserted into the centre of the cakes comes out clean. Let the cakes cool in the tins for 5 minutes before turning out onto a wire rack to cool completely.

2   Cut out the body pieces from the template, position on the cakes and secure each piece with a toothpick. Cut the cakes to shape, then remove the template and toothpicks. Slice the leg piece in half lengthways so that it is half the thickness of the other pieces. Discard one half of the leg. Assemble the cake on the cake board as shown, joining the pieces with a little of the ganache.

3   Tint 2 tablespoons of the ganache bright orange. Tint the remainder of the ganache pale pink. Transfer 2 tablespoons of the pink ganache to a small bowl and tint darker pink for the ears and tail. Cover the cake with a thick layer of the pale pink ganache, leaving the tail and centre of the ears un-iced (un-frosted). Make soft waves in the ganache with a palette knife. Ice (frost) the centres of the ears and the tail with the darker pink ganache.

4   Put the carrot on the cake board in front of the rabbit and ice (frost) it with orange ganache. Make cuts in the spearmint leaf three quarters of the way through to resemble the leafy top of a carrot. Attach to the top of the carrot.

5   Slice the marshmallow in half horizontally and stick half in place for the nose. Put the chocolate melts in a heatproof bowl. Bring a saucepan of water to the boil, then remove from the heat. Sit the bowl over the pan, making sure the base of the bowl does not touch the water. Stir occasionally until the chocolate has melted. Pipe eight chocolate lines of various lengths on a tray lined with baking paper — you will only need four but it is good to have extra. Leave the whiskers for 5–10 minutes to set. Then, stick the four whiskers in place. Give the rabbit an eye by using a pink sugar-coated chocolate lolly. Use one mini mint for a buck tooth, and another four for claws. Draw on the mouth with a skewer.

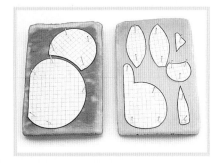
Stick all the template pieces into position on the two cakes.

Piece the rabbit together, then join all the pieces with a little ganache.

Pipe eight thin lengths of melted chocolate onto a tray covered with baking paper.

volcano vesuvius

1 In a large bowl, combine 210 g (7½ oz/7 cups) of the puffed rice cereal and 45 g (1¾ oz/½ cup) of the coconut, then sift in 60 g (2¼ oz/½ cup) of the cocoa powder and 215 g (7¾ oz/1¾ cups) of the icing sugar. Mix together and make a well in the centre. Melt 350 g (12 oz) of the Copha in a saucepan over low heat. Pour into the well and mix together. Spoon the mixture into the pudding basin and refrigerate for 4 hours, or until hard and set. Turn out the chocolate mixture onto the cake board.

2 Make the same quantity of chocolate mixture again and cool completely. Once cool, use the extra mixture to build up the shape of the volcano, moulding with your hands. Supporting the top of the volcano with one hand, scoop out a hollow in the top of the volcano with a spoon — this will be the crater. Put the volcano in the refrigerator to set.

3 Put the chocolate in a heatproof bowl. Bring a saucepan of water to the boil, then remove from the heat. Sit the bowl over the pan, making sure the base of the bowl does not sit in the water. Stir occasionally until the chocolate has melted. Cut long strips of fruit strap, narrower at the top, wider at the bottom, to represent flowing lava. Stick to the sides of the volcano — you shouldn't need to use anything to stick it on, but if you are transporting the cake, use a little melted chocolate. Drizzle some of the melted chocolate down the sides of the volcano. Stick chunks of rocky road, honeycomb and chocolate onto the volcano with a dab of melted chocolate so that they will stay in place. Just before serving, scrunch up some cellophane and stick it into the crater to look like billowing flames.

CAKE AND EQUIPMENT

420 g (15 oz/14 cups) puffed rice cereal

90 g (3¼ oz/1 cup) desiccated coconut

125 g (4½ oz/1 cup) unsweetened cocoa powder

430 g (15¼ oz/3½ cups) icing (confectioner's) sugar

700 g (1 lb 9 oz/3 cups) Copha (white vegetable shortening)

2 litre (70 fl oz/8 cups) pudding basin (mould)

35 cm (14 inch) square cake board

DECORATION

150 g (5½ oz/1 cup) chopped dark chocolate

red and orange fruit straps

85 g (3 oz/3/4 cup) broken rocky road

100 g (3½ oz) honeycomb

100 g (3½ oz) chocolate bar with triangular pieces, broken

red and yellow cellophane

NOTE

If you are going to transport this cake, put the finished cake in the refrigerator for at least 30 minutes before travelling so that the chocolate mixture is nice and hard. If it is a hot day, take a bottle of self-hardening chocolate sauce to stick on any 'rocks' that might fall off.

Spoon the chocolate mixture into the pudding basin.

Build up the shape of the volcano with the extra chocolate mixture.

Stick the pieces of honeycomb onto the volcano, securing with melted chocolate.

little miss ladybird

CAKE AND EQUIPMENT

24 cm (9½ inch) round cake tin
2 packets cake mix
35 cm (14 inch) square cake board
copy of template from page 136
toothpicks
ruler

DECORATION

1½ quantities buttercream from page 11
food colourings: light brown and red
1 metre (3 ft) long liquorice strap
giant sugar-coated chocolate lollies
    (candies)

NOTE
We have been creative with our
ladybird; if you want her to be more
realistic, use black lollies (candies) for
the spots and create only three sets
of legs.

1   Preheat the oven to 180°C (350°F/Gas 4). Grease the cake tin and line with
    baking paper. Pour the cake mix into the tin and bake for 35–40 minutes,
    or until a skewer inserted into the centre of the cake comes out clean.
    Let the cake cool in the tin for 5 minutes before turning out onto a wire
    rack to cool completely.

2   Sit the cake on the cake board, position the template of the body on the cake
    and secure with toothpicks. Cut the cake to shape. Remove the template and
    toothpicks. Turn one of the offcuts on its side, put the head template on it and
    cut to shape. Repeat with the other offcut so that you have two bits of head.
    Put the two head sections on top of each other, sticking them together with a
    little buttercream.

3   To shape the body into a dome, shave all around the cake with a large serrated
    knife, as shown. Position the cake on the cake board and attach the head to
    the body with a little buttercream. Use a small, sharp knife to round the top of
    the head.

4   Reserve 2 tablespoons of the buttercream and tint it caramel brown. Tint the
    remainder of the buttercream bright red and ice (frost) the body with it. Next,
    ice (frost) the head with the brown buttercream.

5   Cut a 27 cm (10¾ inch) long piece of liquorice and split the bottom third of
    the strap into two thin strips. Lay the liquorice strip along the centre of the
    body with the split at the tail end — this is the wing parting. Cut the remaining
    liquorice into thin strips and cut about twelve very short pieces, about 1–2 cm
    (½–¾ inches) from the strip to make the eyes. Next, cut eight 5 cm (2 inch)
    lengths out of the liquorice strips for the legs. Stick the eyes and legs in place.

6   Dot giant sugar-coated chocolate lollies all over the body and cut one of the
    red lollies in half for the mouth — if they don't stick to the icing (frosting), dab
    the bottom of them with a little extra buttercream.

Turn the offcut onto its side and cut
around the head template with a knife.

Once the head is in position, round out
the top with a small, sharp knife.

Using a palette knife, ice (frost) the head with the light brown buttercream.

Split the bottom third of the liquorice strap in two.

Use a skewer to transfer the wing pattern onto the cake.

Join the butterfly pieces together with some buttercream.

Sprinkle the centre of the wing with the rainbow choc chips.

beautiful butterfly

1   Preheat the oven to 180°C (350°F/Gas 4). Grease the cake tins and line the bases with baking paper. Divide the cake mix evenly between the tins and bake for 25–30 minutes, or until a skewer inserted into the centre of the cakes comes out clean. Let the cakes cool in the tins for 5 minutes before turning out onto a wire rack to cool completely.

2   Sit the cakes on the cake board, put the template pieces into position and secure with toothpicks. Use a skewer or toothpick to mark the wing pattern onto the cake by piercing through the paper.

3   Cut out the body pieces, then the wings. Remove the template and toothpicks. Move the pieces together into the shape of a butterfly and join with a little buttercream.

4   Leave half the buttercream white and tint the remaining buttercream with a few drops of red food colouring. Ice (frost) the body and the centre section of the wings with the white buttercream. Cut the liquorice into thin strips and outline the wing pattern. Cover the centre of the wings with the rainbow choc chips.

5   Spread pink buttercream over the rest of the butterfly and make slight furrows in the pink buttercream with a palette knife.

6   Decorate the edge of the butterfly's wings with mini jubes. Use two dark coloured jubes for the eyes. Put the chocolate melts in a heatproof bowl. Bring a saucepan of water to the boil, then remove from the heat. Sit the bowl over the pan, making sure the base of the bowl does not sit in the water. Stir occasionally until the chocolate has melted. Spoon the chocolate into a piping bag. Pipe two feelers onto a sheet of baking paper, allow to set, then stick into the top of the body, just underneath the eyes.

CAKE AND EQUIPMENT
two 20 x 30 cm (8 x 12 inch) rectangular cake tins
3 packets cake mix
35 x 45 cm (14 x 18 inch) cake board
2 copies of template from page 137
toothpicks or skewers

DECORATION
1½ quantities buttercream from page 11
red food colouring
1 metre (3 ft) long liquorice strap
130 g (4¾ oz/¾ cup) rainbow choc chips
mini jubes (gumdrops)
35 g (1¼ oz/¼ cup) dark chocolate melts (buttons)

tropical fish

CAKE AND EQUIPMENT
two 22 cm (8½ inch) round cake tins
2 packets cake mix
copy of template from page 138
toothpicks or skewers
40 x 55 cm (16 x 22 inch) cake board

DECORATION
1½ quantities buttercream from page 11
food colourings: red and blue
blue and purple sprinkles (sugar
   strands)
3–4 liquorice ropes
red cake decorating gel
1 round mint
sugar-coated chocolate lollies (candies)
rainbow choc chips

1 Preheat the oven to 180°C (350°F/Gas 4).
Grease the cake tins and line the bases with baking
paper. Divide the cake mix evenly between the tins and
bake for 25–30 minutes, or until a skewer inserted into
the centre of the cakes comes out clean. Let the cakes cool
in the tins for 5 minutes before turning out onto a wire rack
to cool completely.

2 Level the cakes if necessary. Position the body template on
one cake and secure with toothpicks. Mark the stripes onto
the cake by piercing through the paper with a skewer or
toothpick. Using a small, sharp knife, cut out the mouth.
Remove the template and toothpicks. Cut out the other pieces
of the template and place on the other cake as shown and secure
with toothpicks. Cut out the pieces.

3 Assemble the fish on the cake board as shown, rounding out the fins if they
need it so that they join the body neatly.

4 Put half the buttercream in one bowl and a quarter each into two smaller
bowls. Tint the larger portion pink, tint one quarter blue and leave the rest of
the buttercream white.

5 Spread the white buttercream onto the face. Ice (frost) the middle stripe, tail
and the air bubbles with the blue buttercream. Attach the fins to the cake by
butting them against the blue stripe. Ice (frost) the first and third stripes and
the fins with the pink buttercream.

6 Fill one saucer with blue sprinkles and one with purple and dip an air bubble
into each until they are well coated.

7 Outline the stripes and accent the tail with liquorice ropes. Pipe around the
edge of the mouth with red gel. Create an eye with the mint and a chocolate
lolly: use a dab of any leftover buttercream to stick them together, and put
into place. Decorate the fish's stripes with the sugar-coated chocolate lollies.
To finish, sprinkle rainbow choc chips on the tips of the tail.

Mark the stripes onto the cake by piercing
through the template with a skewer.

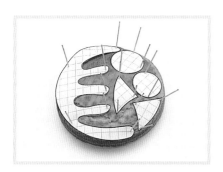

Put the other template pieces on the second cake and secure with toothpicks.

Make the shape of the fish with the pieces of cake.

Outline the fish's mouth with red cake decorating gel.

Return the cake to the roasting tin, sitting it over the set jelly.

Carefully pull the foil off the jelly, but don't worry if a little of it sticks to the foil.

Spread the buttercream around the sides of the cake.

reef-world aquarium

1   Preheat the oven to 180°C (350°F/Gas 4). Grease the tin and line the base with baking paper. Pour the cake mix into the tin and bake for 40–45 minutes, or until a skewer inserted into the centre of the cake comes out clean. Let the cake cool in the tin for 5 minutes before turning out onto a wire rack to cool completely. Once cool, cover the cake in plastic wrap.

2   Clean the roasting tin and line it with foil; lightly oil the foil. Make up the jelly according to the packet instructions and pour into the tin. Refrigerate for about 6 hours, or until set.

3   Lay the crackers out on a work surface and use a pastry brush to dust off any flavouring powder. Turn the sharks over so the white side is facing up and trim the blue side so that they will sit flat. Paint the crackers with food colouring and draw patterns on the sharks with a toothpick dipped in colouring.

4   Using a sharp knife, cut the snake into pieces about 7 cm (2¾ inches) long — try to get two colours on each piece. Holding one end of each length, make two splits in the other end. Fan out the cut sections to resemble coral or seaweed.

5   Unwrap the cake, level it if necessary and take the jelly out of the refrigerator. Put the cake, bottom-side-down, on the jelly. Hold the cake board over the cake and carefully invert the tin so that the cake is on the bottom and the jelly turns out onto the cake. Carefully peel back the foil — use a small knife to ease the jelly from the foil around the edges, if necessary.

6   Tint the buttercream with a few drops of the blue food colouring and spread it around the sides of the cake, coming right up the sides of the jelly. Swirl the buttercream with a palette knife so that it looks like swirling water.

7   Sprinkle the rainbow choc chips along the bottom of the jelly. Cut the shell chocolates in half along the seam, and add to the cake. Put the coral in place, then arrange the fish. Refrigerate until required (don't cover); the cake will keep for up to 18 hours in the refrigerator.

CAKE AND EQUIPMENT
20 x 30 x 5 cm (8 x 12 x 2 inch) roasting tin
2 packets cake mix
2 x 85 g (3 oz) packets blue jelly (gelatin dessert) crystals
1 pastry brush or small paintbrush
toothpicks
30 x 40 cm (12 x 16 inch) cake board

DECORATION
fish-shaped crackers
3 lolly (candy) sharks
food colourings: red, blue and yellow
1 giant multi-coloured snake or different coloured snakes
½ quantity buttercream from page 11
rainbow choc chips
2–4 chocolate shells, at room temperature (see Note)

NOTE
Because the chocolates get cut along the seam, you only need two chocolates, but we used four for added variety.

spotty the dog

CAKE AND EQUIPMENT

19 cm (7¹/₂ inch) square cake tin

22 cm (8¹/₂ inch) round cake tin

2 packets cake mix

copy of template from page 139

toothpicks

30 x 45 cm (12 x 18 inch) cake board

DECORATION

2 quantities buttercream from page 11

2 tablespoons unsweetened cocoa
   powder, sifted

100 g (3¹/₂ oz/³/₄ cup) grated dark
   chocolate

1 chocolate-coated biscuit (cookie)

white and pink marshmallows

sugar-coated chocolate lollies (candies)

1 metre (3 ft) long liquorice strap

small dog collar (see Note)

NOTE

We have used a real collar, but if
you want to make a lolly (candy) collar,
place a piece of liquorice strap under
the dog's chin and secure sugar-coated
chocolate lollies (candies) to it with a
little buttercream.

1 Preheat the oven to 180°C (350°F/Gas 4). Grease the cake tins and line the bases with baking paper. Divide the cake mix evenly between the tins and bake the square cake for 35–40 minutes, then the round cake for 35–40 minutes, or until a skewer inserted into the centre of the cakes comes out clean. Let the cakes cool in the tins for 5 minutes before turning out onto a wire rack to cool completely.

2 Level the cakes if necessary. Cut out the templates of the ears and stick on the square cake with toothpicks. Cut out the head template and secure it to the round cake. Cut the cakes to shape, then remove the templates and toothpicks. Transfer the cake to the cake board, push the ears against the head and attach them with a little buttercream.

3 Put one third of the buttercream into a bowl, add the cocoa and beat well. Use the remaining white buttercream to spread over the dog's face and ears, leaving odd-shaped gaps here and there — these will be filled with chocolate buttercream to represent the spots.

4 Use the chocolate buttercream to fill in the un-iced (un-frosted) gaps. Smooth the buttercream on the face and rough up the buttercream on the ears with a knife. Gently press the grated chocolate onto the spots.

5 Stick the chocolate biscuit in the middle of the face for the nose. To make the eyes, cut a white marshmallow in half and stick a blue sugar-coated chocolate lolly onto each half with a little buttercream. Stick the eyes just above the nose. Trim the rounded end off a halved pink marshmallow for the tongue and put it slightly below the nose. Cut the liquorice into thin strips, then cut three short lengths of liquorice for the eyebrows and tongue and two longer pieces for the snout. Place them into position, then snip tiny pieces of liquorice for the spots around the nose and sprinkle them onto the cake. Add a red sugar-coated chocolate lolly at the top of the tongue. Sit the collar below the head.

Sit the cake on a board and join the ears to the head with some buttercream.

Spread the white buttercream over the dog, leaving gaps for the chocolate spots.

To make a lolly collar, add a strap of liquorice with lollies stuck to it.

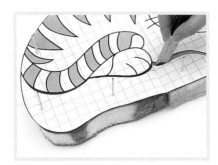

Separate the mat from the cake by cutting the cake along the split section.

Spread violet buttercream over the mat with a palette knife.

Fill in the cat's stripes by piping dark orange buttercream into them.

cat on a mat

1 Preheat the oven to 180°C (350°F/Gas 4). Grease the cake tins and line the bases with baking paper. Divide the mixture evenly between the tins and bake for 45–50 minutes, or until a skewer inserted into the centre of the cakes comes out clean. Let the cakes cool in the tins for 5 minutes before turning out onto a wire rack to cool completely.

2 Set aside $^1/_2$ cup of the buttercream for the white areas. Tint 1 cup of the buttercream violet for the mat and tint the remainder pale orange (using a combination of red and yellow) for the body. Get two smaller bowls and put $^1/_4$ cup of the orange buttercream in one bowl and ¾ cup in another. Tint the smaller portion medium orange and the larger portion dark orange.

3 Level the top of the cakes, then place them on the cake board, joining the edges with a little buttercream. Cut out the template, then cut along the line which separates the cat's body from the mat. Position the two pieces of template on the cake and secure with toothpicks. Cut around the edge of the template, then cut along the edge of the mat so that the cake is in two pieces — this will make the icing (frosting) easier to do. Remove the templates and toothpicks.

4 Spread the violet buttercream over the mat. Spread the pale orange buttercream all over the cat's body, then join the two pieces of cake together with some of the buttercream.

5 Using the template as a reference, mark all the cat's stripes onto the icing (frosting) with a skewer or toothpick. Transfer the darkest orange buttercream to a piping bag and fill in the dark orange stripes, using your skewer marks as a guide. Smooth the buttercream with a small palette knife.

6 Spread white buttercream in the ear areas, mouth area and tips of the tail and paws and blend softly into the pale orange buttercream so that you don't end up with sharp lines. Draw all the cat's remaining features onto the icing (frosting) with a skewer — these will help you with the piping.

7 Put the medium-coloured orange buttercream into a small piping bag and pipe over your skewer marks to outline the cat's body, head, tail, claws and around the stripes — but don't do the features that will be marked in chocolate.

8 Put a jellybean in position for the nose. Melt the chocolate as described on page 9, spoon into a piping bag and pipe the eyes, mouth and paws with melted chocolate, following the skewer marks. Pipe whiskers onto a sheet of baking paper. When set, lift into place. Drop silver dragées around the whiskers.

CAKE AND EQUIPMENT
two 23 cm (9 inch) square cake tins
3 packets cake mix
25 x 40 cm (10 x 16 inch) cake board
copy of template from page 140
toothpicks or skewers

DECORATION
2$^1/_2$ quantities buttercream from page 11
food colourings: violet, red and yellow
1 red jellybean
50 g (1¾ oz/$^1/_3$ cup) dark chocolate
   melts (buttons)
silver dragées or cachous

fatty the whale

CAKE AND EQUIPMENT
two 20 x 30 cm (8 x 12 inch)
   rectangular cake tins
3 packets cake mix
50 cm (20 inch) square cake board
copy of template from page 141
toothpicks or skewers

DECORATION
1½ quantities meringue frosting
   from page 11
food colourings: blue and red
1 metre (3 ft) long liquorice strap
marshmallows
1 blue sugar-coated chocolate lolly
   (candy)
egg white
blue and green sprinkles (sugar strands)

1   Preheat the oven to 180°C (350°F/Gas 4). Grease the cake tins and line the bases with baking paper. Divide the mixture evenly between the tins and bake for 20–25 minutes, or until a skewer inserted into the centre of the cakes comes out clean. Let the cakes cool in the tins for 5 minutes before turning out onto a wire rack to cool completely.

2   Sit the cakes on the cake board and join the long edges with a little frosting. Level the cakes if necessary. Cut out the pieces of the template, position them on the cake and secure with toothpicks. Looking at the picture to help you, mark the lines between different coloured icings (frostings) onto the cake by piercing through the paper onto the cake with a skewer or toothpick. Cut the cakes to shape with a small, sharp knife. Remove the template and toothpicks.

3   Put the whale on the cake board, move the fins and waterspout into place and attach with a little frosting.

4   Reserve one third of the meringue frosting and tint the remaining frosting blue. Spread the blue frosting over the areas you have marked out with the skewer, leaving the undercarriage, mouth, spot and spout un-iced (un-frosted).

5   Take 2 tablespoons of the remaining white meringue frosting, add a drop of red colouring and use this pink frosting to fill in the mouth. Use the remaining white frosting to ice (frost) the undercarriage of the whale, the spot and the spout, peaking the frosting on the spout to represent water.

6   Cut the liquorice into long thin strips. Outline the blue part of the whale and the mouth with liquorice strips. Cut a marshmallow in half and stick a blue sugar-coated chocolate lolly on top (securing it with a little frosting) and put in place for the eye. Add a small strip of liquorice for the eyebrow. To make air bubbles, dip marshmallows in egg white and coat with sprinkles.

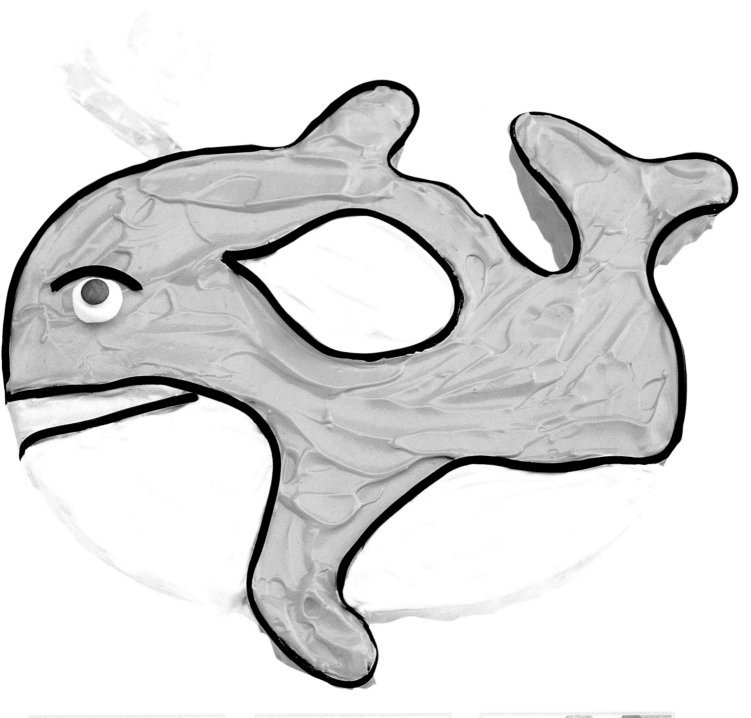

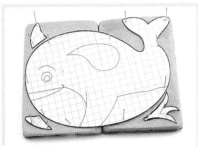

Position the template pieces on the joined cakes and secure with toothpicks.

Place the cake pieces into position and join with a little of the frosting.

Spread the frosting over the body of the whale with a palette knife.

mini cakes

Pick your four favourite mini cake designs and make six of each. Preheat the oven to moderate 180°C (350°F/Gas 4). Use one packet of cake mix and fill two 12-hole standard muffin tins two thirds full. Bake for 20 minutes, or until a skewer inserted into the centre comes out clean. Cool, then decorate. You will need a half quantity of buttercream (see page 11) to ice (frost) 24 mini cakes.

lovely ladybird

Tint 2 tablespoons of the buttercream pale pink with 1 drop of red food colouring. Spread onto the cakes. Put a chocolate melt (button) in the centre of the cake. Using imitation chocolate cake decorating gel, pipe spots, face, head and wing parting onto the ladybird. Make legs out of thin strips of liquorice. Decorate the cake with silver dragées or cachous. Makes 6.

frog in a pond

Tint 2 tablespoons of buttercream with 4–5 drops blue food colouring. Spread onto the cakes. Tint 1 tablespoon desiccated coconut with 1 drop green colouring and add to one side. Sit a frog on top. Makes 6.

purring pussycat

Tint 2 tablespoons buttercream orange with 2 drops yellow and 1 drop red food colouring. Use a pink lolly (candy) to make the nose. Position the nose and make whiskers from banana lollies (candies). Draw the mouth with imitation chocolate cake decorating gel. Halve a green sugar-coated chocolate lolly (candy) and position on the cake for the eyes. Snip a pink marshmallow in half and position on the cake for the ears. Pinch the tops to make pointy ears. Makes 6.

flower power

Lightly whisk 1 egg white. Using a paint brush, paint non-sprayed rose petals with a little egg white. Sprinkle with caster (superfine) sugar. Sit on a wire rack to set (about 30 minutes). Spread 2 tablespoons buttercream over the cakes and top with sugared petals. Line the edges of the cake with dragées or cachous. Makes 6.

well-dressed bear

Spread 2 tablespoons chocolate buttercream over the patty cakes. Halve 1 brown sugar-coated chocolate lolly (candy) and position, cut-side-up, for the eyes. Cut a black jellybean in half for the nose. Trim a piece of liquorice to form the mouth and larger pieces for the ears. Use an orange lolly (candy) to make the bow tie. Makes 6.

swinging cherries

Tint 2 tablespoons buttercream pale pink with 1–2 drops of red food colouring. Cut glacé cherries in half. Cut spearmint leaf (candied fruit leaf) in half lengthways and trim to make small leaves. Ice (frost) the cakes, position the cherries and make stems by cutting thin pieces of liquorice. Press on the leaves. Makes 6.

prickly porcupine

Spread the cakes with chocolate buttercream. Arrange small strips of liquorice for the spikes. Cut black jellybeans in half and stick, round-side-up, for the eyes. Use a trimmed bullet (liquorice bean/torpedo) for the nose. Makes 6.

be my valentine

Tint 2 tablespoons of buttercream pale pink with 1 drop red food colouring. Ice (frost) the cakes and stick a heart-shaped chocolate in the centre. Makes 6.

tiger stripes

Tint 2 tablespoons of buttercream orange with 2 drops of yellow and 1 drop of red food colouring. Trim pieces of liquorice strap to make the eyes, nose, mouth and ears. Cut thin strips from the orange and black part of liquorice allsorts (striped liquorice candies) and position around the edges of the cake to make the stripes. Makes 6.

sunny sunflower

Roll out apricot compressed fruit bars to 5 mm (1/4 inch) thick. Cut out petals with a small, sharp knife. Tint 2 tablespoons plain buttercream with 2 drops of yellow food colouring. Ice (frost) the cake and arrange the petals on the cake leaving a small circle in the middle. Fill the circle with chocolate sprinkles (sugar strands). Makes 6.

snake in the grass

Tint 2 tablespoons of the buttercream bright green. Put 2 tablespoons shredded coconut in a small bowl and add 2 drops green food colouring. Stir well until the coconut turns green. Ice (frost) the cupcakes with green icing (frosting) and sprinkle with a little coconut. Put a snake lolly (candy) on the cake and sprinkle with a little coconut. Makes 6.

marshmallow flower

Tint 2 tablespoons of buttercream blue with 4—5 drops blue food colouring. Snip a pink or white marshmallow in half and arrange in a petal pattern. Put a sugar-coated chocolate lolly (candy) in the centre. Makes 6.

out and
about

fighter plane

CAKE AND EQUIPMENT

two 20 x 30 cm (8 x 12 inch)
  rectangular cake tins
3 packets cake mix
copy of template from pages 142–143
45 x 60 cm (18 x 24 inch) cake board
toothpicks

DECORATION

2 quantities buttercream from page 11
food colourings: black and red (we used
  powder)
liquorice allsorts (striped liquorice
  candies)
1 short liquorice strap
6 blue or black bullets (liquorice
  beans/torpedoes) or lollies (candy)

1 Preheat the oven to 180°C (350°F/Gas 4). Grease the cake tins and line the bases with baking paper. Divide the cake mix evenly between the tins and bake for 25–30 minutes, or until a skewer inserted into the centre of the cakes comes out clean. Let the cakes cool in the tins for 5 minutes before turning out onto a wire rack to cool completely.

2 Tint ¼ cup of the buttercream black and tint the remaining buttercream bright red. Cut out the template pieces, position on the cakes as shown and secure with toothpicks. Cut the cakes to shape and remove the templates and toothpicks.

3 Assemble the bottom layer of the cake on the cake board as shown. Join the nose and tail sections together with a little buttercream, attach the wings to either side of the back part of the nose section, then attach the back wings at the end of the plane's body. Ice (frost) this layer red.

4 Shave the cockpit into a dome shape and cover the front section with black buttercream but leave the rest un-iced (un-frosted). Assemble the top layer by sitting the cockpit over the nose and joining the cabin to the back of the cockpit. Ice (frost) the rest of the top layer red, then sit the tail on top of the end of the plane and ice (frost) it red.

5 Cut out ten black liquorice pieces from liquorice allsorts and stick them on the cake as the plane's windows. Cut crosses out of the liquorice strap and position on the wings. Press the bullets into the front of the wings — these will be the guns.

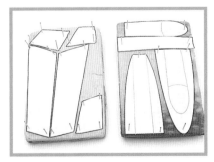

Secure the template pieces onto the cakes with toothpicks.

Join the front wings and the back wings to the side of the bottom layer.

Using a small, sharp knife, shave the cockpit area into a dome.

dumpy the tip truck

1 Preheat the oven to 180°C (350°F/Gas 4). Grease the cake tins and line the bases with baking paper. Divide the cake mix evenly between the tins and bake for 40–45 minutes, or until a skewer inserted into the centre of the cakes comes out clean. Let the cakes cool in the tins for 5 minutes before turning out onto a wire rack to cool completely.

2 Cut the lid off an egg carton and trim the edges if necessary so that it will sit flat. Wrap the lid in foil and sit it on the cake board, cut-edge-down — this will support the cake and elevate it. Level one of the cakes, then cut it in half horizontally. With one of the halves of the cake, leave a 1.5 cm (⁵/₈ inch) border all around and scoop out a shallow hollow — this will be the 'tray' of the tip truck.

3 Cut one third off the other loaf cake. Stand the short piece on its cut side on the front of the egg carton. Stand the longer piece behind the first piece so that together they look like the bonnet and cabin of the truck. Sit the intact cake half behind the cabin on the back of the egg carton. Join the pieces together with a little buttercream.

4 Put one third of the buttercream in a bowl and leave it white for the white areas. Tint the remaining buttercream bright red. Spread the red buttercream over the truck, leaving the windscreen, windows and tray un-iced (un-frosted). Cut the chocolate bars in half diagonally through the long side and place evenly in a line on the base of the truck. This will support the tray of the truck. Put the tray on top of the chocolate bars and ice (frost) with the white buttercream. Next, fill in the spaces left for the windows and windscreen with white buttercream.

5 Outline the windows and bonnet with thin strips of liquorice and put handles on the doors. Use chocolate-coated biscuits for the wheels. Trim the ice cream wafer to fit and place it on front of the truck as the grille. Decorate as shown, then fill the tray of the truck with assorted lollies.

CAKE AND EQUIPMENT

two 11 x 18.5 cm (4¼ x 7½ inch) loaf (bar) tins
2 packets cake mix
1 cardboard egg carton
15 x 30 cm (6 x 12 inch) cake board

DECORATION

1½ quantities buttercream from page 11
red food colouring (we used powder)
2 chocolate-coated caramel snack bars
1 metre (3 ft) long liquorice strap
6 round chocolate-coated biscuits (cookies)
1 ice cream wafer
250 g (9 oz/1½ cups) assorted lollies (candies)

Using scissors, cut an egg carton in half; discard the base.

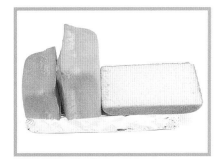

Assemble the tip truck on the foil-covered egg carton.

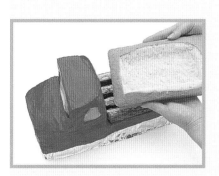

Sit the tray of the tip truck on top of the layer of chocolate bars.

gnarly dude! skateboard

CAKE AND EQUIPMENT

20 x 30 x 5 cm (8 x 12 x 2 inch)
  rectangular roasting tin
2 packets cake mix
4 x 8 cm (3¼ inch) chocolate rolls
20 x 35 cm (8 x 14 inch) cake board
copy of template from page 144
toothpicks
ruler

DECORATION

35 g (1¼ oz/¼ cup) dark chocolate
  melts (buttons)
35 g (1¼ oz/¼ cup) white chocolate
  melts (buttons)
1½ quantities buttercream from page 11
food colourings: green and violet
long green fruit straps
4 dark-coloured sugar-coated
  chocolate lollies (candies)

1 Preheat the oven to 180°C (350°F/Gas 4). Grease the roasting tin and line the base with baking paper. Pour the cake mix into the tin and bake for 35–40 minutes, or until a skewer inserted into the centre of the cake comes out clean. Cool in the tin for 5 minutes before turning out onto a wire rack to cool completely.

2 Melt the dark and white chocolate melts separately as described on page 9. Draw some sticker designs onto a sheet of non-stick baking paper. Lightly oil a baking tray, and turn the paper onto it so that the pencil marks are underneath and the images are backwards.

3 Put the melted dark chocolate into a small paper piping bag, and pipe over the pencil lines. Leave until set. Fill in the outlines with melted white chocolate — the chocolate should be fairly thick but even. Refrigerate until set.

4 Using a serrated knife, level the cake if necessary, then turn over. Position the template on the cake and secure with toothpicks. Cut the cake to shape. Remove the template and toothpicks. Cut down into the blunt end of the skateboard at a 45-degree angle — the small wedge will become the tail.

Once the dark chocolate has set, fill in the outlines with melted white chocolate.

Cut a wedge off the blunt end of the skateboard and keep the wedge.

Put an extra piece of cake in between the wheels to act as extra support.

5   Tint ³/₄ cup of the buttercream pale green. Ice (frost) each of the rolls with
    green buttercream, but leave one end of each un-iced (un-frosted). Put
    two rolls on the cake board with the un-iced (un-frosted) ends 1 cm (¹/₂ inch)
    apart, and sit the other pair parallel, 11 cm (4¹/₄ inches) away. Put a piece of
    leftover cake, the same height as the rolls, in the gap between the rolls as
    support for the cake.

6   Tint the remaining buttercream dark violet and cover the skateboard with it.
    Carefully lift the skateboard onto the wheels. Sit the wedge on the end of the
    skateboard and cover with violet buttercream.

7   Cut four 30 cm (12 inch) lengths from the fruit straps. Press two together,
    one on top of the other, then repeat with the other two. Trim one end of
    each strap on a slight angle to fit the front of the skateboard. Run the two
    strips parallel down the centre of the board. Lift the chocolate 'stickers' from
    the tray and place on the skateboard, right-side-up. Put a sugar-coated lolly in
    the centre of each wheel.

electric guitar

1. Preheat the oven to 180°C (350°F/Gas 4). Grease the cake tins and line the bases with baking paper. Divide the cake mix evenly between the tins and bake for 40–45 minutes, or until a skewer inserted into the centre of the cakes comes out clean. Let the cakes cool in the tins for 5 minutes before turning out onto a wire rack to cool completely.

2. Cut one of the cakes into thirds lengthways and leave the other whole. Position as shown on the cake board, joining the edges with buttercream. Put the template on the cake and secure with toothpicks. Mark the centre area, which will be iced (frosted) with white buttercream, onto the cake by piercing through the paper with a skewer. Cut the guitar to shape. Remove the template. Trim the guitar's neck if it is too wide. Using one of the offcuts, add some extra length to the guitar's neck, joining with buttercream. Trim the end into a curve. Put 1/2 cup of the white buttercream in a bowl and leave white. Put another 1/2 cup in a bowl and mix with the cocoa powder. Tint the remaining buttercream buttery orange with yellow and red colourings.

3. Ice (frost) the middle part of the guitar with white buttercream, using your skewer marks as a guide. Next, ice (frost) a 10 cm (4 inch) tip at the end of the neck and the rest of the guitar's body with yellow buttercream. Ice (frost) the rest of the neck with brown buttercream. Cut the liquorice into strips and outline the white part of the guitar with a thin strip of liquorice.

4. Use six pieces of chocolate and six chocolate lollies of the same colour for the tuning machines and tuning pegs. Cut out two 1 x 7 cm (1/2 x 2¾ inch) long strips of liquorice. Lie them across the middle of the cake and add a chocolate bullet on either end of them. Cut the liquorice strap into six thin strips approximately 55 cm (22 inches) long and run them along the length of the guitar for the strings, starting at the first liquorice strip and ending where the yellow buttercream on the neck begins. Put a strip of liquorice over the end of the strings at the neck end. Decorate the guitar with the remaining lollies and halved marshmallow as shown.

CAKE AND EQUIPMENT
two 20 x 30 cm (8 x 12 inch) rectangular cake tins
3 packets cake mix
30 x 80 cm (12 x 32 inch) cake board
copy of template from page 145
toothpicks or skewers
ruler

DECORATION
2½ quantities buttercream from page 11
food colourings: yellow and red
1 tablespoon unsweetened cocoa powder, sifted
2 x 1 metre (3 ft) long liquorice straps
1 chocolate bar with triangular pieces
sugar-coated chocolate lollies (candies)
4 chocolate bullets (liquorice beans/torpedoes)
1 marshmallow

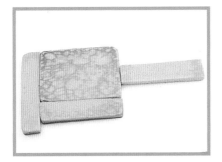

Join the cake strips to the main cake in the basic shape of a guitar.

After you have added an extra piece to the end of the neck, cut it into a curve.

Stick six pieces of chocolate on the end of the guitar.

vroom vroom racing car

CAKE AND EQUIPMENT

20 x 30 cm (8 x 12 inch) rectangular
   cake tin
10 x 21 x 5 cm (4 x 8¼ x 2 inch) loaf
   (bar) tin
2 packets cake mix
25 x 30 cm (10 x 12 inch) cake board
copy of template from page 146
toothpicks

DECORATION

1½ quantities buttercream from page 11
food colourings: red, yellow and blue
2 x 1 metre (3 ft) long liquorice straps
1 yellow musk stick (candy stick)
8 round chocolate biscuits (cookies)
4 mints
2 mini jubes (gumdrops/fruit pastilles)
2 liquorice twists
1 marshmallow
liquorice allsorts (striped liquorice
   candies)
2 yellow aniseed domes

1 Preheat the oven to 180°C (350°F/Gas 4). Grease the cake tins and line the bases with baking paper. Divide the cake mix evenly between the tins and bake for 40–45 minutes, or until a skewer inserted into the centre of the cakes comes out clean. Let the cakes cool in the tins for 5 minutes before turning out onto a wire rack to cool completely.

2 Put the template of the chassis onto the rectangular cake and secure with toothpicks. Cut to shape, then remove the template and toothpicks. Shape the loaf by shaving a slice off either side of the cake so that the sides taper in. Next, starting from almost halfway along the cake, shave the front at about a 45-degree angle.

3 Put ¼ cup of the buttercream in a small bowl and tint it bright orange by combining red and yellow food colourings. Tint the rest of the buttercream bright blue. Put the chassis in the middle of the cake board and cover with blue buttercream. Lift the body of the car onto the chassis, then ice (frost) it with blue buttercream.

4 Pipe narrow stripes of orange buttercream down the centre and sides of the car and run thin strips of liquorice between the stripes. Shape a car number from the musk stick (you could use liquorice instead) and attach to the front of the car.

5 To make a wheel, sandwich two of the chocolate biscuits together with a little buttercream and wrap 18 cm (7 inch) of liquorice strap around the outside, securing with a trimmed toothpick (make sure you remove the toothpicks before serving). Repeat with the other biscuits so that there are four wheels. Attach a mint to the centre of each wheel with a little buttercream and position the wheels on the car.

6 To make the rear spoiler, push a toothpick through a 4 cm (1½ inch) liquorice twist, through one end of a 10 cm (4 inch) liquorice strap and into a jube. Repeat on the other end of the strap and stick onto the car (again, remove the toothpicks before serving).

7 Use a marshmallow as the helmet. Add details with thin strips of liquorice and liquorice allsorts. Use the aniseed domes for headlights.

Cut a diagonal slice off the front sides of the cake, then a larger slice off the front.

Lay thin strips of liquorice between the piped stripes of orange.

Wrap a liquorice strip around each pair of chocolate biscuits.

Make the rear spoiler by threading a toothpick through a liquorice twist.

speed demon rollerblade

1 Preheat the oven to 180°C (350°F/Gas 4). Grease the cake tin and line the base with baking paper. Pour the cake mix into the tin and bake for 40–45 minutes, or until a skewer inserted into the centre of the cake comes out clean. Cool in the tin for 5 minutes before turning out onto a wire rack to cool completely.

2 Level the cake if necessary. Cut the cake in half, then cut one third off one of the halves. To assemble the cake, add the shortest piece to the top of the longest, then use the remaining piece for the toe. Join the pieces together with buttercream.

3 Trim the edges of the toe and heel so that the edges are rounded. Next, cut a shallow crescent from the back of the ankle. Finally, cut a small triangular strip off the top of the boot. Turn this triangular strip over to stand on its side and trim if necessary to make it the same height as the rest of the cake. Join the triangle to the top of the boot with a little buttercream.

4 Tint ½ cup of the buttercream black, ½ cup orange and tint the remaining buttercream bright green. Ice (frost) the heel and very top of the boot black. Next, ice (frost) a decorative orange stripe in the middle and finally, ice (frost) the rest of the boot bright green.

5 To make the wheels, sandwich pairs of biscuits together with a little buttercream and line them along the base of the cake. Put a long strip of liquorice over the top of the wheels, securing with a little buttercream. Cut the ends of the liquorice into a sharp angle and stick a black sugar-coated chocolate lolly on top of each pair of wheels with a dab of buttercream.

6 To finish, put three strips of liquorice of varying lengths on the boot to represent buckles. Cut one curved edge off three blue sugar-coated chocolate lollies and stick the flat edge of one against each boot buckle. Cut four very thin strips of liquorice for the laces and position as shown, finishing with a mini jube on each end. Cover each of the joins between buttercream colours with a thin strip of liquorice, and add one strip to the middle of the orange part.

CAKE AND EQUIPMENT
19 cm (7½ inch) square cake tin
1 packet cake mix
30 x 40 cm (12 x 16 inch) cake board
toothpicks

DECORATION
2 quantities buttercream from page 11
food colourings: black, green and
   orange (we used powder for black)
8 round chocolate-coated biscuits
   (cookies)
1 metre (3 ft) long liquorice strap
black and blue sugar-coated chocolate
   lollies (candies)
4 red mini jubes (gumdrops/fruit
   pastilles)

Cut the cake in half, then cut one third off the end of one of the pieces.

Sit the triangular offcut on its side at the top of the boot.

Stick biscuits together with buttercream so that you have four wheels.

choo-choo train

CAKE AND EQUIPMENT

two 9 x 22 x 6 cm (4 x 9 x 3 inch)
   loaf (bar) tins
1½ packets cake mix
15 x 55 cm (6 x 22 inch) cake board
2 x 5 cm (2 inch) jam rollettes (mini
   jelly rolls)
ruler
56 ice block sticks or coffee stirrers

DECORATION

2 quantities buttercream from page 11
food colourings: red, blue and green
1 metre (3 ft) long liquorice strap
1 large white marshmallow
250 g (9 oz/1½ cups) assorted lollies
   (candies)
18 chocolate jewels (chocolate
   nonpareils/rainbow drops)

1   Preheat the oven to 180°C (350°F/Gas 4). Grease the cake tins and line the
    bases with baking paper. Divide the cake mix evenly between the tins and bake
    for 35–40 minutes, or until a skewer inserted into the centre of the cakes
    comes out clean. Let the cakes cool in the tins for 5 minutes before turning
    out onto a wire rack to cool completely.

2   Level the cakes if necessary. Cut one third off one cake and cut the other cake
    into three even pieces.

3   To make the track, line up five ice block sticks end to end along the cake board.
    Line up another five sticks parallel to the first track. Lay single ice block sticks
    across the tracks.

4   To make the engine, sit one of the small pieces of cake on top of the large
    piece and position on the train track. Use the rollettes to make the train funnel
    as shown. To make the carriages, turn the cake pieces upside down and, using a
    small, sharp knife, hollow out each piece to a depth of 1.5 cm (⅝ inch), leaving
    a 1 cm (½ inch) border. Line up the carriages on the track behind the engine.

5　Divide the buttercream in half and tint one portion blue. Divide the remaining buttercream into thirds and tint one portion red, one portion purple (by mixing blue and red together) and one portion green. Ice (frost) the engine with the blue buttercream, but use one of the other colours for the funnel. Ice (frost) each of the wagons a different colour.

6　Cut the liquorice strap into thin strips and outline the engine and wagons. Put a marshmallow on the engine's funnel to resemble smoke.

7　Position two chocolate jewels along the bottom of each side of the wagons and three along each side of the engine carriage for the wheels. Decorate the train with some of the assorted lollies, then generously fill the wagons with them.

Cut one third off one cake and cut the other one into three equal pieces.

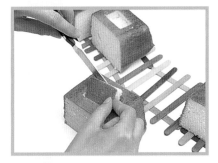

Hollow out each carriage piece, leaving a border, before icing (frosting).

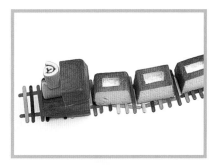

Assemble the cake pieces as shown, lining the carriages behind the engine.

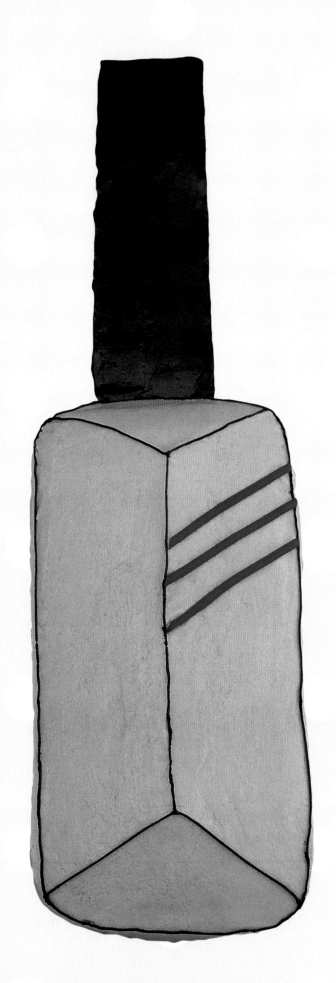

cricket bat and ball

1 Preheat the oven to 180°C (350°F/Gas 4). Grease the cake tins and line the bases with baking paper. Divide the mixture evenly between the tins and bake for 20–25 minutes, or until a skewer inserted into the centre of the cakes comes out clean. Let the cakes cool in the tins for 5 minutes before turning out onto a wire rack to cool completely.

2 Cut out the blade and handle templates, position on one of the cakes and secure with a couple of toothpicks. Using a small, sharp knife, cut the cake to shape. Lift the shaped blade (with the template still stuck to it) onto the second cake and align the long edges. Cut the second cake to shape. Use the cutter to cut out a round from the second cake — this will become the cricket ball. Remove the templates and toothpicks and spread some buttercream between the two cakes making up the blade.

3 Using a serrated knife, shape the blade cake into the shape of a house roof by shaving off both long sides diagonally on a 45-degree angle from the centre to the edges of the cake. Next, slice a 5 cm (2 inch) slope from each short end of the cake.

4 Join the handle to the top of the blade cake to make a cricket bat. Shave the round of cake into a ball with a small sharp knife.

5 Tint 1¼ cups of the buttercream caramel brown, ¼ cup red, leave 1 tablespoon white and tint the remainder black. Ice (frost) the blade of the bat with the brown buttercream. Reserve 2 tablespoons black buttercream and use the rest to ice (frost) the handle. Ice (frost) the ball with the red buttercream. Put the white buttercream in a small piping bag and pipe stitching onto the ball. Put the reserved black buttercream in a small piping bag and outline the cricket bat. Cut out three 7 cm (2¾ inch) strips of red liquorice and add decorative strips to the bat.

CAKE AND EQUIPMENT
two 20 x 30 cm (8 x 12 inch) rectangular cake tins
2 packets cake mix
copy of template from page 147
toothpicks
7 cm (2¾ inch) round biscuit (cookie) cutter
25 x 45 cm (10 x 18 inch) cake board
ruler

DECORATION
1 quantity buttercream from page 11
food colourings: caramel, red, black and green (we used powder for red)
red liquorice laces

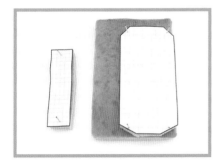

Align the base of the blade along one edge of the second cake.

Shave down the sides of the top cake on a 45-degree angle.

Join the handle to one end of the bat with some buttercream.

the fun boat

CAKE AND EQUIPMENT

two 11 x 21 x 7 cm (4 x 8 x 3 inch)
   loaf (bar) tins
1½ packets cake mix
ruler
20 x 35 cm (8 x 14 inch) cake board
toothpicks

DECORATION

1½ quantities of buttercream from
   page 11
food colourings: red, yellow and blue
coloured popcorn
fruit rings
sugar-coated chocolate lollies (candies)
mini jubes (gumdrops/fruit pastilles)
2 x 1 metre (3 ft) long liquorice straps

1   Preheat the oven to 180°C (350°F/Gas 4). Grease the loaf tins and line the bases with baking paper. Divide the cake mix evenly between the tins and bake for 40–45 minutes, or until a skewer inserted into the centre of the cakes comes out clean. Let the cakes cool in the tins for 5 minutes before turning out onto a wire rack to cool completely.

2   Put two thirds of the buttercream in a small bowl and tint it bright red. Divide the remaining buttercream in two, with one portion larger than the other. Add blue to the larger portion and yellow to the other.

3   Stand the cakes right-side-up. Slice a 5 cm (2 inch) piece from the short ends of one cake (Cake 1), then slice these end pieces horizontally with one piece slightly larger than the other — the larger pieces will become the second deck and the smaller pieces will become the top deck. Cut the other cake (Cake 2) in half and slice the outside corners off on an inward slant.

4   Trim the pieces of cake that will become the top deck so that they are shorter and thinner than the pieces for the deck below. Use the triangular offcuts to cut three cubes for the funnels for the top of the boat.

5   Put the large piece from Cake 1 between the two triangular pieces from Cake 2. Line up the bottom of the two ends from Cake 1 end to end. Do the same with the smaller pieces for the top deck. Move the middle deck onto the top of the bottom deck and the top deck on top of that. Finish with the funnels.

6   Once the cake is assembled, take apart piece by piece to ice (frost) the bottom deck red, the middle deck blue and the top deck yellow. Ice (frost) the funnels blue and reassemble cake on the cake board.

7   Thread three pieces of popcorn onto each toothpick, trimming the end of the toothpick with scissors (remember to remove the popcorn and toothpicks before serving). Press into the tops of the funnels. Decorate the boat with the lollies as shown. Make an anchor out of thin liquorice and line the top and bottom of each deck with liquorice strips.

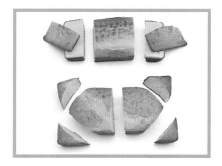

Cut the ends off cake 1 and slice them in half; cut cake 2 in half and trim the corners.

Line each of the decks up on the cake board in front of you.

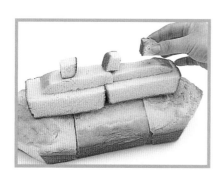

Assemble the ship, each deck centred over the one below.

cartoon fun

bart simpson

CAKE AND EQUIPMENT
two 20 x 30 cm (8 x 12 inch)
   rectangular cake tins
3 packets cake mix
35 x 40 cm (14 x 16 inch) cake board
copy of template from page 148
toothpicks or skewers

DECORATION
1½ quantities buttercream from page 11
food colourings: red, black and yellow
   (we used powder for red and black)
2 x 1 metre (3 ft) long liquorice straps
1 black jellybean

1 Preheat the oven to 180°C (350°F/Gas 4). Grease the cake tins and line the bases with baking paper. Divide the cake mix evenly between the tins and bake for 25–30 minutes, or until a skewer inserted into the centre of the cakes comes out clean. Let the cakes cool in the tins for 5 minutes before turning out onto a wire rack to cool completely.

2 Sit the cakes on the cake board and join the long edge of one to the long edge of the other with some buttercream. Attach the template to the cake with toothpicks, then cut to shape. Mark the eyes and mouth onto the cake by piercing through the paper with a skewer or toothpicks. Remove the template and toothpicks.

3 Reserve ⅓ cup of the buttercream for the eyes. Tint 1 tablespoon of the remaining buttercream dark red for the tongue and another tablespoon black for the inside of the mouth — you will only need a small amount of powder for each. Tint the remaining buttercream bright yellow.

4 Spread the yellow buttercream evenly over the cake, using your skewer marks to show you where to leave the eyes and mouth un-iced (un-frosted). Use a palette knife to make vertical furrows for the hair. Next, ice (frost) the eyes with white buttercream. Transfer the red and black buttercream to separate piping bags and ice (frost) the mouth as shown. Once the buttercream is in place, smooth it with a palette knife.

5 Cut the liquorice into thin strips, then use these to outline the cake and the features of the face. Cut the jellybean in half and position round-side-up as pupils for the eyes.

Cut the cake to shape and mark the feature lines with a skewer.

Ice (frost) the face yellow, leaving the eyes and mouth un-iced (un-frosted).

Pipe the black and red buttercream for the mouth, then smooth with a palette knife.

MATT GROENING

MATT GROENING

marge simpson

1 Preheat the oven to 180°C (350°F/Gas 4). Grease the cake tins and line the bases with baking paper. Divide the cake mix evenly between the tins and bake for 25–30 minutes, or until a skewer inserted into the centre of the cakes comes out clean. Let the cakes cool in the tins for 5 minutes before turning out onto a wire rack to cool completely.

2 Sit the cakes on the cake board and join the short edge of one cake to the short edge of the other with some buttercream. Position the template on the cake as shown and secure with toothpicks. Use a skewer or toothpick to transfer the hairline and eyes onto the cake by piercing through the paper — these lines will help you when you are icing (frosting) the cake. Cut the cake to shape. Remove the template and toothpicks.

3 Tint ¼ cup of the buttercream black, leave ¼ cup white and tint 1 cup bright yellow. Tint the remaining buttercream bright blue.

4 Using your skewer marks as a guide, spread the yellow buttercream over the face, the white buttercream in the eye area and the blue buttercream over the hair. Use a palette knife to create soft swirls in Marge's hair.

5 Copying the template or picture, use a skewer to mark the outlines of the eyes, nose, mouth and ear onto the buttercream — if you make a mistake, you can smooth over these marks and redo them. Use your markings as a guide for piping on the features with black buttercream, then pipe around the hair. To dress Marge, make a necklace out of gum balls.

CAKE AND EQUIPMENT
two 20 x 30 cm (8 x 12 inch)
  rectangular cake tins
3 packets cake mix
25 x 55 cm (10 x 22 inch) cake board
copy of template from page 149
toothpicks or skewers

DECORATION
2½ quantities buttercream from page 11
food colourings: black, yellow and blue
  (we used powder for black)
red gum balls (gobstoppers)

Join the cakes along the short sides, then position the template on the cake.

Use a skewer to draw Marge's features onto the icing (frosting).

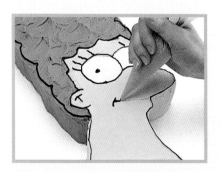

Pipe black buttercream over the guide markings you made for Marge's features.

homer simpson

CAKE AND EQUIPMENT

two 20 x 30 cm (8 x 12 inch)
  rectangular cake tins
3 packets cake mix
35 x 50 cm (14 x 18 inch) cake board
copy of template from page 150
toothpicks or skewers

DECORATION

3 quantities buttercream from page 11
food colourings: yellow, brown, red and
  black (we used powder for red and
  black)
1 large doughnut

1   Preheat the oven to 180°C (350°F/Gas 4). Grease the cake tins and line the
    bases with baking paper. Divide the cake mix evenly between the tins and bake
    for 25–30 minutes, or until a skewer inserted into the centre of the cakes
    comes out clean. Let the cakes cool in the tins for 5 minutes before turning
    out onto a wire rack to cool completely.

2   Sit the cakes on the cake board. Join the long side of one cake to the short side
    of the other with a little buttercream, as shown. If necessary, level the bottom cake
    — the thought cloud doesn't need to be level so you can leave it as it is. Position
    the template on the cake and secure with toothpicks. Mark any lines separating
    different buttercream colours onto the cake by piercing through the paper with
    a skewer or toothpick — these lines will show you where to spread the
    buttercream. Cut the cake to shape, then remove the template and toothpicks.

3   Tint 1 cup of the buttercream bright yellow, 1/2 cup dark mustard yellow
    (by blending a couple of drops of yellow with quite a lot of the brown),
    1 tablespoon deep red and 1/2 cup black. Leave the remaining buttercream white.

4   Spread the buttercream evenly over the cake using the skewer marks
    as a guide. Start by icing (frosting) the eyes, shirt and thought cloud white.
    Then, spread yellow buttercream over the head and mustard yellow over
    the jaw. To finish the icing (frosting), put the red and black buttercream
    into separate piping bags and pipe red buttercream into the bottom of
    the mouth and black buttercream into the top of the mouth area. Smooth the
    buttercream with a palette knife.

5   With the template or picture as a reference, use a skewer to mark the outlines
    and features onto the icing (frosting). Pipe over these marks with black
    buttercream. Next, pipe the outline of some thought bubbles (if you are
    using a coloured cake board, fill in the thought bubbles with some white
    buttercream). Carefully pipe some drool from his mouth. Finally, add
    Homer's fantasy doughnut to the middle of the thought cloud.

Position the cakes on the cake board,
joining them with buttercream.

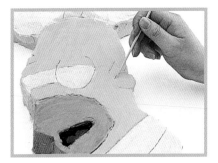

Use a skewer to mark Homer's features
onto the icing (frosting).

Pipe over your skewer outlines with black
buttercream.

MATT GROENING

MATT GROENING

lisa simpson

1 Preheat the oven to 180°C (350°F/Gas 4). Grease the cake tins and line the bases with baking paper. Divide the cake mix evenly between the tins and bake for 25–30 minutes, or until a skewer inserted into the centre of the cakes comes out clean. Let the cakes cool in the tins for 5 minutes before turning out onto a wire rack to cool completely.

2 Sit the cakes on the cake board and join the long edge of one cake to the long edge of the other with some buttercream. Position the template on the cake and secure with toothpicks. Use a skewer or toothpick to mark any lines between different colours onto the cake by piercing through the paper. Cut the cake to shape. Remove the template and toothpicks.

3 Leave ¼ cup of the buttercream white. Tint ½ cup of the buttercream bright red. Tint the remaining buttercream bright yellow.

4 Spread the yellow buttercream over the cake using the skewer marks to show you where to leave un-iced (un-frosted). Next, ice (frost) the dress red and, finally, fill in the eyes with white buttercream. Cut long thin strips of liquorice and use to outline the eyelashes, eyes, ear, dress, nose and mouth. Use more of the liquorice to outline the edges of the cake.

5 To dress Lisa, make a necklace out of gum balls and position as shown. Cut the jellybean in half and place round-side-up as the pupils.

CAKE AND EQUIPMENT
two 20 x 30 cm (8 x 12 inch)
  rectangular cake tins
3 packets cake mix
30 x 40 cm (12 x 16 inch) cake board
copy of template from page 151
toothpicks or skewers

DECORATION
2 quantities buttercream from page 11
food colourings: red and yellow (we
  used powder for red)
5 large white gum balls (gobstoppers)
  or white chocolate balls
2 x 1 metre (3 ft) long liquorice straps
1 black jellybean

Make the outline of the eyes and dress onto the cake.

Once you have iced (frosted) the face, fill in the eyes with white buttercream.

Cut a jellybean in half and press, round-side-up, into Lisa's eyes.

maggie simpson

CAKE AND EQUIPMENT

two 20 x 30 cm (8 x 12 inch)
 rectangular cake tins
3 packets cake mix
30 x 40 cm (12 x 16 inch) cake board
copy of template from page 152
toothpicks or skewers

DECORATION

2 quantities buttercream from page 11
food colourings: red, blue and yellow
 (we used powder for red)
2 x 1 metre (3 ft) long liquorice straps
1 black jellybean

1 Preheat the oven to 180°C (350°F/Gas 4). Grease the cake tins and line the bases with baking paper. Divide the cake mix evenly between the tins and bake for 25–30 minutes, or until a skewer inserted into the centre of the cakes comes out clean. Let the cakes cool in the tins for 5 minutes before turning out onto a wire rack to cool completely.

2 Sit the cakes on the cake board and join the long edge of one cake to the long edge of the other with some buttercream. Position the template on the cake as shown, secure with toothpicks and cut the cake to shape. Referring to the picture, mark any lines separating different coloured icings (frostings) onto the cake by piercing through the paper with a skewer or toothpick — these lines will help you when you are spreading on the icing (frosting). Remove the template and toothpicks.

3 Reserve 2 tablespoons of white buttercream for the eyes. Tint 1/4 cup of the buttercream dark red for the pacifier. Divide the remaining buttercream in half and tint one portion bright blue and the other bright yellow.

4 Spread the yellow buttercream over the hands and face, leaving the eye area un-iced (un-frosted). Next, cover the baby outfit with blue buttercream. Fill in the area for the eyes with white buttercream. Using a skewer, mark the outline of the pacifier and hair bow onto the icing (frosting). Put the remaining blue buttercream in a piping bag and pipe on the bow, then smooth with a palette knife. Put the red buttercream in a piping bag and fill in the area you have marked out for the pacifier. Smooth the buttercream with a palette knife.

5 Cut the liquorice straps into thin strips and use to outline the features and the edges of the cake. Cut the jellybean in half and position round-side-up for the pupils.

Use a small knife to cut around the edge of the template.

Fill the space for the eyes with white buttercream.

Outline Maggie and her features with thin strips of liquorice.

MATT GROENING

MATT GROENING

santa's little helper

1 Preheat the oven to 180°C (350°F/Gas 4). Grease the cake tins and line the bases with baking paper. Divide the cake mix evenly between the tins and bake for 25–30 minutes, or until a skewer inserted into the centre of the cakes comes out clean. Let the cakes cool in the tins for 5 minutes before turning out onto a wire rack to cool completely.

2 Sit the cakes on the cake board and join the long edge of one cake to the long edge of the other with some buttercream. Position the template on the cake, secure with toothpicks and cut the cake to shape. Transfer the outline of the eyes and nose onto the cake by piercing through the paper with a skewer or toothpick. Remove the template and toothpicks. Attach the tail to the board by spreading some of the buttercream underneath the cake.

3 Reserve 1–2 tablespoons of white buttercream for the eyes. Tint 3 tablespoons of the buttercream black. Tint the remaining buttercream an orange brown colour by blending brown and red food colourings.

4 Spread the buttercream evenly over the cake using the skewer marks as a guide — white for the eyes, black for the nose and brown for the rest of the cake. You might find it easier to ice (frost) the nose and eyes first.

5 Copying from the template or picture, draw the features onto the icing (frosting) with a skewer — if you make a mistake, smooth over the lines and redo them. Carefully pipe over these marks with black buttercream.

CAKE AND EQUIPMENT

two 20 x 30 cm (8 x 12 inch)
    rectangular cake tins
3 packets cake mix
35 x 40 cm (14 x 16 inch) cake board
copy of template from page 153
toothpicks or skewers

DECORATION

1½ quantities buttercream from page 11
food colourings: red, brown and black
    (we used powder for black)

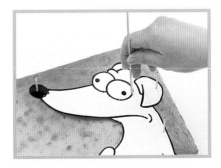

Pierce through the template with a skewer to outline the eyes and nose.

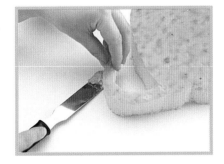

Secure the tail to the cake board with a little buttercream.

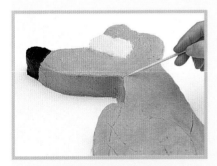

Mark the features onto the icing (frosting) with a skewer.

mr. montgomery burns

CAKE AND EQUIPMENT

two 20 x 30 cm (8 x 12 inch)
   rectangular cake tins
3 packets cake mix
30 x 45 cm (12 x 18 inch) cake board
copy of template from page 154
toothpicks or skewers

DECORATION

3 quantities buttercream from page 11
food colourings: yellow, red, black and
   green (we used powder for red, but
   liquid for black to achieve grey)

1　Preheat the oven to 180°C (350°F/Gas 4). Grease the cake tins and line the bases with baking paper. Divide the cake mix evenly between the tins and bake for 25–30 minutes, or until a skewer inserted into the centre of the cakes comes out clean. Let the cakes cool in the tins for 5 minutes before turning out onto a wire rack to cool completely.

2　Put the cakes together on a cake board as shown, joining the edges with a little buttercream. Position the template on the cake and secure with toothpicks. Mark any lines separating different icing (frosting) colours onto the cake by piercing through the paper with a skewer or toothpick. Cut the cake to shape, then remove the template and toothpicks.

3　Reserve 1/3 cup white buttercream for the eyes, shirt and teeth. Tint 1 1/2 cups buttercream bright yellow, 2 tablespoons deep red, 1/2 cup grey using a little of the black food colouring, and the remaining buttercream bright green for the jacket.

4　Using your skewer marks as a guide, ice (frost) Mr. Burns with white buttercream for the eyes, mouth, shirt and cuffs. Then, use yellow buttercream for the hands and head and smooth with a palette knife. Spread grey buttercream over the hair but leave about 3 tablespoons of the grey for later. Use the green buttercream for the jacket. Next, transfer the red buttercream to a piping bag and pipe it onto the tie. Use 1 tablespoon of the reserved grey buttercream to pipe on the spots on the head.

5　Tint the remaining grey buttercream black by adding more black colouring. Copying the template or picture, use a skewer to mark the features of the face and body onto the icing (frosting) — if you make a mistake, smooth them over and start again. Pipe over these markings and the outline with black buttercream.

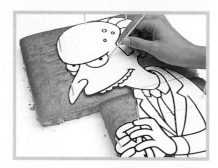

Transfer the features from the template onto the cake by piercing with a skewer.

Spread the buttercream onto the cake with a palette knife

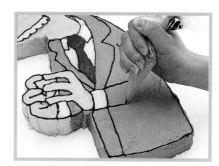

Using your skewer marks as a guide, pipe the features with black buttercream.

MATT GROENING

MATT GROENING

head to toe bart simpson

1 Preheat the oven to 180°C (350°F/Gas 4). Grease the cake tins and line the bases with baking paper. Divide the cake mix evenly between the tins and bake for 25–30 minutes, or until a skewer inserted into the centre of the cakes comes out clean. Let the cakes cool in the tins for 5 minutes before turning out onto a wire rack to cool completely.

2 Sit the cakes on the cake board and join the long edge of one cake to the long edge of the other with some buttercream. Position the template on the cake and secure with toothpicks. Use a skewer or toothpick to mark out the lines between icing (frosting) colours onto the cake by piercing through the paper (you will need to refer to the picture to do this). Cut the cake to shape, then remove the template and toothpicks.

3 Put ⅓ cup of the buttercream in a bowl and leave it white. Place ⅔ cup of the buttercream in one bowl and tint it deep red, put ½ cup in another bowl and tint deep blue and tint ½ cup black. Tint the remaining large quantity bright yellow.

4 Spread the buttercream evenly over the cake using the skewer marks as a guide — white for the eyes; yellow for the head, arms and legs; blue for the shorts and shoes and red for the T-shirt. Put the remaining white buttercream in a small piping bag and pipe the white buttercream quite thickly over the shoe soles, side dots and socks.

5 Copying the template or picture, outline the features with a skewer, then pipe over your skewer marks with black buttercream. Next, pipe around the edges of the cake. To finish Bart, add two dots of black buttercream for the pupils of his eyes.

CAKE AND EQUIPMENT

two 20 x 30 cm (8 x 12 inch) rectangular cake tins
3 packets cake mix
35 x 45 cm (14 x 18 inch) cake board
copy of template from page 155
toothpicks or skewers

DECORATION

3 quantities buttercream from page 11
food colourings: red, blue, black and yellow (we used powder for red and black)

Mark out the lines between icing (frosting) colours with a skewer.

Using your skewer marks as a guide, ice (frost) Bart with a palette knife.

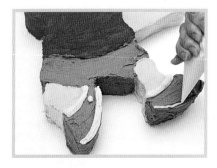

Add detailing to Bart's shoes by piping with white buttercream.

itchy & scratchy

CAKE AND EQUIPMENT
two 20 x 30 cm (8 x 12 inch)
   rectangular cake tins
3 packets cake mix
40 cm (16 inch) square cake board
copy of template from page 156
toothpicks or skewers

DECORATION
2 quantities buttercream from page 11
food colourings: yellow, blue, black and
   red (we used powder for red but
   liquid for black to get grey)
2 x 1 metre (3 ft) long liquorice straps
2 black jellybeans
2 mini white marshmallows, cut in half

1 Preheat the oven to 180°C (350°F/Gas 4). Grease the cake tins and line the bases with baking paper. Divide the cake mix evenly between the tins and bake for 25–30 minutes, or until a skewer inserted into the centre of the cakes comes out clean. Let the cakes cool in the tins for 5 minutes before turning out onto a wire rack to cool completely.

2 Sit the long edge of each cake next to one another on a cake board, with the cake on the right slightly lower than the cake on the left. Join the edges with buttercream. Put the template on the cake, secure with toothpicks and cut the cake to shape. Referring to the picture, transfer any lines between different icing (frosting) colours onto the cake by piercing through the paper with a skewer or toothpick. Remove the template and toothpicks.

3 Using about 1 tablespoon of white buttercream, spread the buttercream in the area marked out for Itchy's (the mouse's) eyes. Tint ¾ cup of the buttercream blue and spread all over Itchy's face.

4 Next, move on to Scratchy (the cat). Tint 1½ tablespoons of the buttercream a pale yellow and fill in the eyes. Tint 1 tablespoon of the buttercream red and set it aside. Tint 2 tablespoons of the buttercream pale grey and set it aside. Tint the remaining buttercream dark grey. Spread the dark grey buttercream over Scratchy's face, leaving 1 tablespoon for later use. Next, spread the red buttercream into the area for the tongue. To finish, spread the light grey buttercream into the area for Scratchy's nose. Use the remaining dark grey buttercream to ice (frost) Itchy's nose, then smooth all the buttercream with a palette knife.

5 Cut the liquorice straps into thin strips and outline the whole cake and the features as shown. Cut two jellybeans in half and position round-side-up as the pupils of the eyes. Place the halved marshmallows in place for the fangs/teeth.

Sit the cakes side by side; the one on the left slightly higher than the right.

Pierce the paper with a skewer to mark lines between icing (frosting) colours.

MATT GROENING

Smooth the grey buttercream onto the cake in the area marked out for the nose.

Outline the cake with thin strips of liquorice.

MATT GROENING

Sit the template on the two cakes, then cut off the top right corner.

Move the corner offcut to the bottom of the cake under Krusty's bow tie.

Give the impression of curly hair by softly swirling the green icing (frosting).

krusty the clown

1   Preheat the oven to 180°C (350°F/Gas 4). Grease the cake tins and line the bases with baking paper. Divide the cake mix evenly between the tins and bake for 25–30 minutes, or until a skewer inserted into the centre of the cakes comes out clean. Let the cakes cool in the tins for 5 minutes before turning out onto a wire rack to cool completely.

2   Put the long sides of the two cakes together on a cake board, joining the edges with a little buttercream. Sit the template on the cake and secure with toothpicks — his neck won't fit on yet. Cut off the top right corner of the cake as shown and move underneath Krusty's neck, then join with a little buttercream. Use a skewer or toothpick to mark all the lines between different icing (frosting) colours onto the cake by piercing through the paper — you will need to refer to the picture to do this. Cut the cake to shape, then remove the template and toothpicks.

3   Put ¼ cup of the buttercream in a bowl and leave it white. Put ⅔ cup of the buttercream in a bowl and, adding one drop at a time, tint it very pale yellow. Tint ½ cup of the buttercream caramel. Set five cups next to one another and divide the buttercream among them as follows: the first two cups each have 1 tablespoon of buttercream, then the next three cups each have 2 tablespoons of buttercream. Tint them deep red, grey, purple, blue and black, respectively. Tint the remaining buttercream bright green.

4   Pipe or spread the white buttercream in the areas marked out for the eyes and teeth. Next, spread the yellow buttercream over the neck and the top of the face. Spread the caramel buttercream over the jaw. Spread the red buttercream in the area marked out for the nose and tongue and the grey for inside the mouth. Spread the purple over the collar and carefully make the bow-tie blue. Spread the green buttercream over the hair and swirl with a palette knife to give the impression of curls.

5   Outline all of Krusty's features with a skewer, and, using the skewer marks as a guide, pipe black buttercream over the features and edges of the cake. To finish Krusty, add two dots of black for the pupils of the eyes.

CAKE AND EQUIPMENT
two 20 x 30 cm (8 x 12 inch)
   rectangular cake tins
3 packets cake mix
35 x 45 cm (14 x 18 inch) cake board
copy of template from page 157
toothpicks or skewers

DECORATION
2½ quantities buttercream from page 11
food colourings: yellow, caramel, red,
   grey, purple, blue and black (we used
   powder for red and black)

count to ten

first birthday blocks

CAKE AND EQUIPMENT

two 8 x 25 cm (3¼ x 10 inch) loaf (bar)
  tins
1 packet cake mix
15 x 40 cm (6 x 16 inch) cake board
skewer or toothpick

DECORATION

2 quantities buttercream from page 11
food colourings: red, blue, yellow and
  green

1　Preheat the oven to 180°C (350°F/Gas 4). Grease the cake tins and line the bases with baking paper. Divide the cake mix evenly between the tins and bake for 35 minutes, or until a skewer inserted into the centre of the cakes comes out clean. Let the cakes cool in the tins for 5 minutes before turning out onto a wire rack to cool completely.

2　Level both the cakes. Leave one cake whole and cut the other cake in half, then slice a small triangle off one of the halves. Put the pieces on the cake board in the shape of a one — you will not need the leftover triangle of the cut cake. Join the edges with a little buttercream.

3　Take out four ¼-cup portions of the buttercream and put each into a small bowl. Tint one portion red, another blue, one portion yellow and the final portion green. Spoon each colour into a small piping bag. Leave the largest portion of the buttercream white.

4　Spread white buttercream over the entire surface of the cake, including the sides; spread smoothly with a palette knife. Use a skewer to outline the cubes and mark letters and numbers in the centre of the cubes — we have used random characters but you could use your child's initials.

5　Pipe over your skewer marks on each cube, alternating the colours of the icing (frosting) so that each cube is a different colour. Then, carefully fill in the centre of the letters and numbers with the same colour you used for the outline.

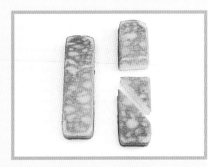

Leave one cake whole and cut the other one into three pieces.

Move the cake into position to form the number one.

Draw the outlines, then fill with matching colour buttercream.

snakey number two

1   Preheat the oven to 180°C (350°F/Gas 4). Grease the cake tins and line the bases with baking paper. Divide the cake mix evenly between the tins and bake for 45 minutes, or until a skewer inserted into the centre of the cakes comes out clean. Let the cakes cool in the tins for 5 minutes before turning out onto a wire rack to cool completely.

2   Do not trim the tops of cakes — leave the cakes rounded to form the shape of a snake. Cut out the pieces of the template and stick on the cakes with toothpicks. Cut the cakes to shape, then assemble cake pieces A–E (from template) into the shape of a snake. Remove the template and toothpicks and join the pieces together with a little buttercream.

3   Put 2 tablespoons of the buttercream in a small bowl and tint it dark violet, similar to the colour of the sprinkles. Spoon the violet buttercream into a piping bag. Tint the remaining buttercream bright green.

4   Spread the green buttercream evenly over the entire cake, using a palette knife to smooth the surface. Once the snake has been completely iced (frosted) with the green buttercream, pipe squiggly patches over the snake with the violet buttercream. Fill the insides of the patches with purple sprinkles.

5   Put the jellybeans in place for the eyes, pipe a little violet buttercream onto the jellybean and stick a purple lolly to the front of it. Pipe a mouth with violet buttercream, then pipe two dots for the nostrils. Make a slit in the head part of the red snake lolly for the tip of the tongue and trim so that it is only about 3 cm (1¼ inches) long. Insert into the mouth of the cake snake.

CAKE AND EQUIPMENT

8 x 25 cm (3¼ x 10 inch) loaf (bar) tin
20 cm (8 inch) ring tin
2 packets cake mix
copy of template from page 158
toothpicks
30 cm (12 inch) square cake board

DECORATION

2 quantities buttercream from page 11
food colourings: violet and green
purple sprinkles (sugar strands)
2 white jellybeans
2 purple sugar-coated chocolate lollies (candies)
1 red snake

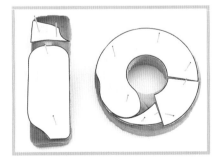

Stick the template pieces onto the cakes with a few toothpicks.

Move the cake pieces into position in the shape of a snake.

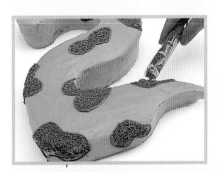

Fill in the outlines you made in violet with purple sprinkles.

third bird-day

CAKE AND EQUIPMENT
two 20 cm (8 inch) ring tins
2 packets cake mix
33 x 33 cm (13 x 13 inch) cake board

DECORATION
1½ quantities buttercream from page 11
food colourings: red and yellow
yellow and white jellybeans
banana lollies
1 marshmallow
1 black jellybean
2 orange snakes

1   Preheat the oven to 180°C (350°F/Gas 4). Grease the cake tins and line the bases with baking paper. Divide the mixture evenly between the tins and bake for 40–45 minutes, or until a skewer inserted into the centre of the cakes comes out clean. Let the cakes cool in the tins for 5 minutes before turning out onto a wire rack to cool completely.

2   Do not level the cakes — leave them rounded. Cut one ring cake in half, with one end pointed for the beak, as shown. Cut a small piece from the middle of the other ring cake. Join the piece with the pointed end to the larger piece in the shape of a the number three.

3   Tint ¼ cup of the buttercream bright orange-red. Tint the remaining buttercream bright yellow. Spread the orange buttercream over the end of the top cake for the beak. Add a couple more drops of red to the leftover orange beak buttercream and ice (frost) a strip along the bottom of the beak for the opening of the mouth. Ice (frost) the rest of the cake with yellow buttercream. Alternatively, you may prefer to ice (frost) all of the cake with the yellow buttercream first and then go over the beak area with the orange buttercream.

4   Cut the jellybeans and bananas in half lengthways. Leave a small space behind the beak for the eyes, then start laying jellybeans over the buttercream, cut-side-down. Stop when you reach the middle point of the three. Stick four rows of bananas in the middle of the cake. Add another five rows or so of jellybeans beneath the bananas, then add another three rows of bananas.

5   Cut a marshmallow in half and make eyes out of it. Cut the ends off a black jellybean and stick rounded-side-up on the marshmallows using a little buttercream to stick them in place. Add plumage by sticking a few bananas at a jaunty angle behind the eyes. Make three slits on the head end of the snakes to create feet and place them on the bottom of the cake as shown. Overlap some bananas on top of the legs to hide the top ends.

Cut the two ring tins into the shapes as shown.

Carefully place the jellybeans on the cake, slightly layering them.

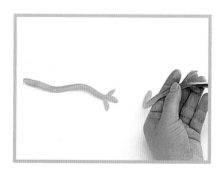

Snip the end of a snake into three thin strips so that they look like bird legs.

race you four it!

1 Preheat the oven to moderate 180°C (350°F/Gas 4). Grease the cake tins and line the bases with baking paper. Divide the mixture evenly among the tins and bake for 35 minutes, or until a skewer inserted into the centre of the cakes comes out clean. Let the cakes cool in the tins for 5 minutes before turning out onto a wire rack to cool completely.

2 Position the cakes on the cake board. Leave one cake whole. Cut the second cake in half, then cut one of the halves in half again. For the last cake, cut a small slice from one end, then cut a triangle off each end of the larger piece. Arrange the cake pieces into the shape of a four on a cake board as shown, levelling the cake if necessary and trimming any pieces that are a little too large. Join the edges with a little buttercream.

3 Reserve ¼ cup of the white buttercream and tint the remaining buttercream caramel brown. Spread the white buttercream over the blaze (the light coloured mark on the face of the horse). Spread brown buttercream over the rest of the horse and blend it neatly into the white icing (frosting).

4 Using a skewer, mark onto the buttercream the mouth, mane, the inside and outside of the ear, and the large comma shape for the nostril. Spread some of the white buttercream into the mouth area, then into the centre of the ear. Build up the height of the outer area of the ear with more brown buttercream.

5 Melt the chocolate as described on page 9. Spoon the melted chocolate into a piping bag, then pipe over your skewer marks to form an outline around the mane, ear and nostril. Fill the mane with chocolate sprinkles. Continue the mane down the side of the cake by pushing sprinkles on the side with a palette knife.

6 To make the eye, stick a brown lolly to a mint with a little buttercream. Cut an eyelash out of a 1.5 cm (⅝ inch) piece of liquorice and put above the eye, fanning out the lashes. Cut thin strips from the liquorice and line the mouth of the horse. Arrange fruit straps for reigns and yellow lollies for the studs.

CAKE AND EQUIPMENT
three 8 x 25 cm (3¼ x 10 inch) loaf (bar) tins
1½ packets cake mix
32 x 32 cm (13 x 13 inch) cake board
ruler

DECORATION
1½ quantities buttercream from page 11
brown food colouring
50 g (1¾ oz/⅓ cup) dark chocolate melts (buttons)
chocolate sprinkles (sugar strands)
1 brown sugar-coated chocolate lolly (candy)
1 round mint
1 short liquorice strap
long red fruit straps
2 yellow sugar-coated chocolate lollies (candies)

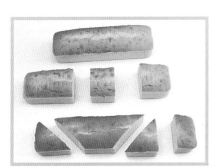

Leave one cake intact and cut the other two as shown.

Move the pieces into the shape of a four and join the pieces with buttercream.

Use a palette knife to push chocolate sprinkles up the side of the cake.

five down on the farm

CAKE AND EQUIPMENT
8 x 25 cm (3¼ x 10 inch) loaf (bar) tin
20 cm (8 inch) ring tin
1½ packets cake mix
25 x 50 cm (10 x 20 inch) cake board
ruler

DECORATION
1½ quantities buttercream from page 11
food colourings: caramel and green
blue cake decorating gel
100 g (3½ oz/⅔ cup) dark or milk
    chocolate melts (buttons)
plastic farm animals or assorted animal
    lollies (candies)

NOTE
If you don't have any farm animals
in the toy box, try the supermarket.
Most supermarkets have a toy section
where you can buy inexpensive toys
that will be perfect for this cake.

1 Preheat the oven to 180°C (350°F/Gas 4). Grease the cake tins and line the bases with baking paper. Divide the cake mix evenly between the tins and bake for 45 minutes, or until a skewer inserted into the centre of the cakes comes out clean. Let the cakes cool in the tins for 5 minutes before turning out onto a wire rack to cool completely.

2 Cut the long cake in half. Cut a piece from the ring cake that is almost a quarter of the ring. Next, square off this piece by neatly cutting off the rounded edges. Arrange the pieces on the cake board in the shape of a five, using the smaller offcuts to lengthen the bar of the number. Join the edges with a little buttercream.

3 Put ¾ cup of the buttercream in a small bowl and tint light brown for the ground cover and tint the remaining buttercream light green for the grass.

4 Mark out three sections for the paddocks and spread green buttercream over the top and bottom sections and brown over the middle section. Make a pond by piping blue food gel onto one of the green paddocks.

5 Put the chocolate in a heatproof bowl. Bring a saucepan of water to the boil, then remove from the heat. Sit the bowl over the pan, making sure the base of the bowl does not sit in the water. Stir occasionally until the chocolate has melted. Spoon the chocolate into a piping bag and create a mud bath for the pigs by piping some of the chocolate into the middle paddock.

6 Pipe the remaining chocolate onto a sheet of baking paper that has been placed on an oiled baking tray. Pipe about 30 fences 3 x 5 cm (1¼ x 2 inch) in size (this will allow for any breakages). When set, carefully stick around the edge of the cake. Decorate the cake with farm animals or lollies of your choice.

Slice off the rounded edges from the side and top of the piece from the ring cake.

Position the cake pieces into the shape of a five.

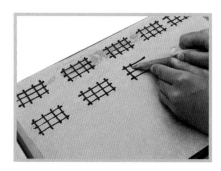
Pipe fences about 3 cm (1¼ in) high and 5 cm (2 in) wide out of melted chocolate.

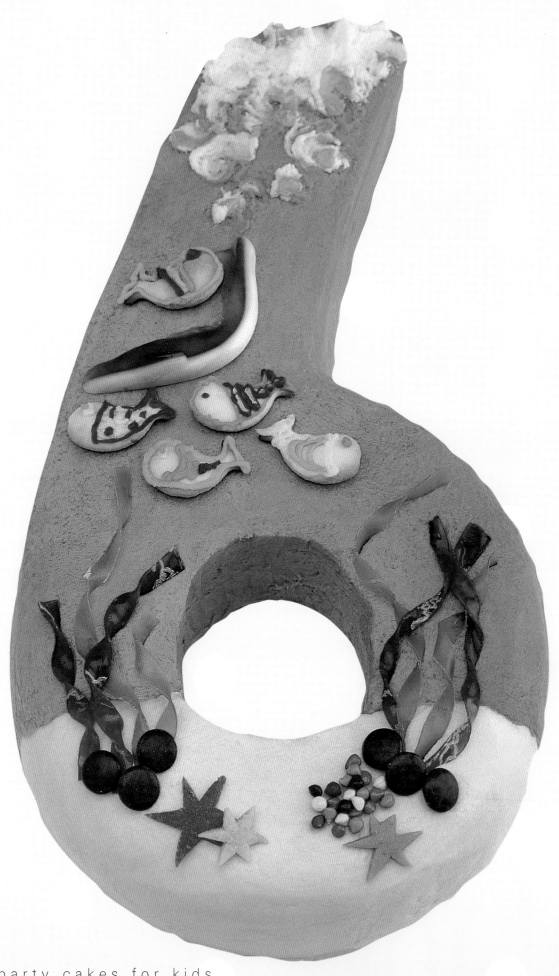

under the sea at six

1 Preheat the oven to 180°C (350°F/Gas 4). Grease the cake tins and line the bases with baking paper. Divide the cake mix evenly between the tins and bake for 45 minutes, or until a skewer inserted into the centre of the cakes comes out clean. Let the cakes cool in the tins for 5 minutes before turning out onto a wire rack to cool completely.

2 Leave the ring cake whole and cut the loaf cake as shown. Arrange the cakes on a cake board in the figure six, discarding the offcuts and joining the edges with a little buttercream. Trim to neaten the edges and the top of the cake.

3 Reserve ¼ cup white buttercream in a small bowl. Place a further ½ cup of buttercream in another bowl and tint caramel to resemble sand. Tint the remaining buttercream blue.

4 Spread sand-coloured buttercream over the bottom of the six and cover the rest of the cake with the blue buttercream. Spread some of the white buttercream at the top to resemble a wave — use a palette knife to rough up the white buttercream so that it looks more realistic.

5 Cut green and red fruit straps into various lengths, then twist the strips a few times so that they look like seaweed strands. Stick the seaweed onto the cake, inserting into the sand-coloured buttercream. Put sugar-coated chocolate lollies at the base of each plant as rockery.

6 Cut the coloured section away from the liquorice allsorts and using a small star cutter or small sharp knife, cut star shapes from them. Put the starfish on the sand. Sprinkle some rainbow choc chips onto the sand to add more colour. Let your imagination run wild and decorate with fish-shaped toys, sweets and crackers, using cake decorating gel or coloured buttercream to make features and patterns on the fish.

CAKE AND EQUIPMENT
8 x 25 cm (3¼ x 10 inch) loaf (bar) tin
20 cm (8 inch) ring tin
1½ packets cake mix
25 x 45 cm (10 x 18 inch) cake board

DECORATION
1½ quantities buttercream from page 11
food colourings: caramel and blue
green and red fruit straps
brown sugar-coated chocolate lollies (candies)
liquorice allsorts (striped liquorice candies)
rainbow choc chips
assorted fish-shaped lollies and sea-themed toys
assorted colours cake decorating gels
goldfish crackers

Cut a sharp curve in the bottom of the loaf cake and a soft curve at the top.

Join the loaf cake to the ring cake with some buttercream.

Add swirls of white buttercream so that it looks like waves crashing on rocks.

seventh heaven

CAKE AND EQUIPMENT

two 8 x 25 cm (3¼ x 10 inch) loaf (bar)
   tins
1 packet cake mix
33 cm (13 inch) square cake board

DECORATION

1½ quantities buttercream from page 11
food colourings: blue and green
2 teaspoons unsweetened cocoa
   powder
150 g (5½ oz/¾ cup) spearmint leaves
   (candied fruit leaves)
2 flaked chocolate bars
banana lollies
toy monkeys or monkey lollies

1   Preheat the oven to 180°C (350°F/Gas 4). Grease the cake tins and line the
    bases with baking paper. Divide the cake mix evenly between the tins and bake
    for 35 minutes, or until a skewer inserted into the centre of the cakes comes
    out clean. Let the cakes cool in the tins for 5 minutes before turning out onto
    a wire rack to cool completely.

2   Trim the cakes as shown so that the top loaf cake has three corners cut off
    (but not the corner that will join the bottom cake), and the second cake
    has a diagonal strip cut off one end and the corners cut off the other end.
    Arrange the pieces on the cake board in the figure seven, joining the
    edges with a little buttercream.

3   Put ¼ cup of the buttercream in a small bowl and tint blue for the sky.
    Divide the remaining buttercream in half. Tint one half green, and add the
    cocoa to the other half and mix together to create a deep brown.

4   Spread a 5 cm (2 inch) strip of blue buttercream at each end of the top of the
    seven and fill in the space with green buttercream. Then, cover the trunk with
    the brown buttercream.

5   Cut the spearmint leaves in half horizontally with sharp scissors and overlap
    on the green buttercream with a few edging over the blue buttercream — it
    looks nice to have the leaves mainly sugar-side-up, but with occasional ones
    shiny-side-up. Break the flaked chocolate bar into flakes and sprinkle over the
    trunk of the tree, pressing down lightly into the buttercream so that they stay
    in place. Arrange assorted bananas in a bunch just below the leaves — we
    used small and large bananas but you can use just one kind if your prefer. For
    the final touch, add your monkeys or other jungle animal to the tree.

Cut the corners off the cakes where shown
and make a diagonal slice off one cake.

Join the cakes together to form the shape
of a seven.

Ice (frost) the sky blue, the leaves green
and the trunk brown.

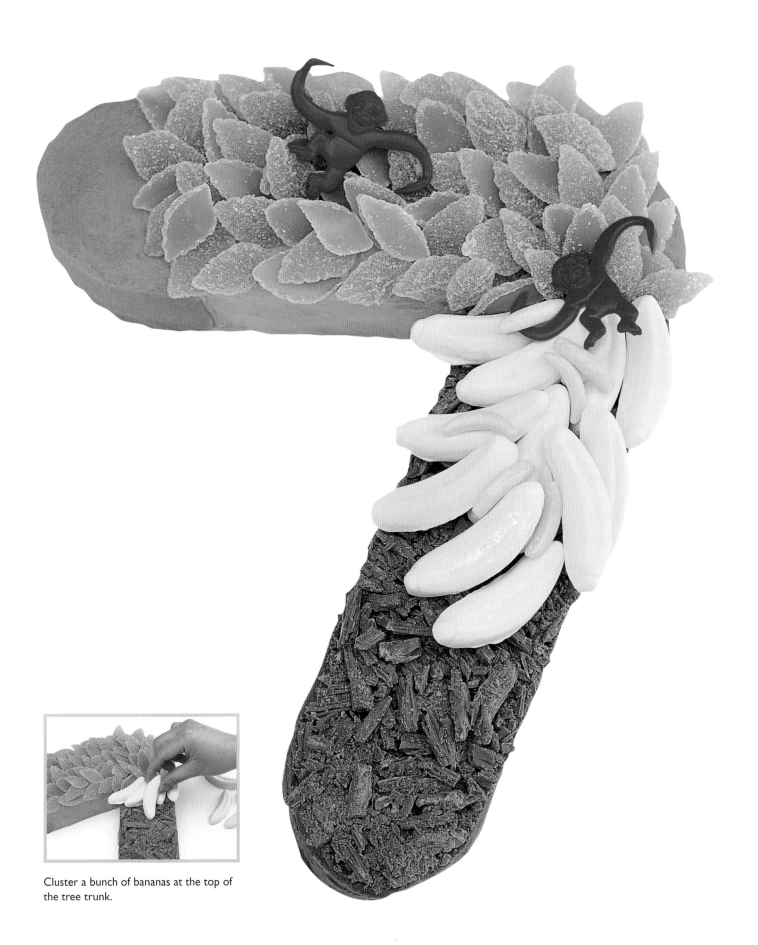

Cluster a bunch of bananas at the top of the tree trunk.

racing at eight

1 Preheat the oven to 180¡C (350¡F/Gas 4). Grease the cake tins and line the bases with baking paper. Divide the cake mix evenly between the tins and bake for 40 minutes, or until a skewer inserted into the centre of the cakes comes out clean. Let the cakes cool in the tins for 5 minutes before turning out onto a wire rack to cool completely.

2 Cut a small slice off each cake as shown so that they will sit flat against each other. Arrange the cakes on the cake board in the figure eight, joining the edges with a little buttercream. Trim to neaten the edges and the top of the cake. Tint the buttercream green, then spread evenly over the cake.

3 Use black liquorice to mark out the lanes of the track and add a strip across the finish line. Cut the red liquorice into short strips about 2 cm (³/4 inch) long (you will need about 35). Put the red strips in a line running down the centre of each lane. Put bear biscuits and jelly babies at the edges of the track for the cheering crowd. Put cars on the track and insert flags (paper or made from toothpicks and liquorice allsort slices) at the finish line and other points around the track.

CAKE AND EQUIPMENT
two 20 cm (8 inch) ring tins
2 packets cake mix
30 x 50 cm (12 x 20 inch) cake board
ruler

DECORATION
2 quantities buttercream from page 11
green food colouring
2 x 1 metre (3 ft) long liquorice straps
red liquorice laces
tiny bear biscuits (cookies)
jelly babies
chocolate or toy cars
flags or liquorice allsorts (striped
  liquorice candies) and toothpicks

Cut a small slice off both of the cakes so that they can sit flat against one another.

Push the cakes together on a cake board and join the edges with buttercream.

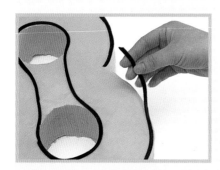

Outline the track with thin strips of black liquorice.

lift off! nine

CAKE AND EQUIPMENT

20 cm (8 inch) ring tin
8 x 25 cm (3¼ x 10 inch) loaf (bar) tin
1½ packets cake mix
25 x 45 cm (10 x 18 inch) cake board

DECORATION

2 quantities buttercream from page 11
food colourings: black and blue (we
    used gel for both)
500 g (1 lb 2 oz) packet ready-made
    icing (frosting)
1 ice cream cone
1 ice cream wafer
dragées or cachous
coloured sprinkles (sugar strands)
red and yellow fruit straps
4 coloured gum balls (gobstoppers)
sugar star decorations

1 Preheat the oven to 180°C (350°F/Gas 4). Grease the cake tins and line the bases with baking paper. Divide the cake mix evenly between the tins and bake for 45 minutes, or until a skewer inserted into the centre of the cakes comes out clean. Let the cakes cool in the tins for 5 minutes before turning out onto a wire rack to cool completely.

2 Leave the ring cake whole and cut a curve from one end of the loaf cake, as shown. Arrange the cakes on a cake board in the figure nine, joining the edges with a little buttercream. Trim to neaten the edges and the top of the cake.

3 Divide the buttercream into six even amounts. Leave one portion white, tint one portion black and tint the others four shades of blue, from light to dark.

4 Spread the buttercream over the cakes, starting with the lighter colours at the bottom and moving up to the darker ones at the top. Blend each colour into the other at the edges.

5 Roll out half the ready-made icing (frosting) with a rolling pin until it is a couple of millimetres thick. Cut out star shapes with a small star cutter or small sharp knife. Cut a circle for a planet.

6 To make the rocket, slice off one side of the cone so that it can sit flat. Spread the rocket with a little white buttercream and roll it on a plate filled with dragées and coloured sprinkles. Carefully fill in any gaps that are left — tweezers makes this job much easier. To make the wings, cut a wafer in half along the diagonal and decorate as above. Sit the rocket's body halfway along the straight part of the nine and slide a wafer wing under each side.

7 Cut the fruit straps into thin strips for the flames and one thin curved strip for the ring around the planet. Add the 'flames' and the gum balls to the bottom of the rocket. Sprinkle the rocket with sugar star decorations. As the final touch, add your stars, planet and planet's ring.

Cut a curve off the top of the loaf cake so that it will neatly join to the ring.

Join the loaf cake to the ring cake to form the figure nine.

Use a small knife or cutter to cut stars out of the ready-made icing (frosting).

Roll the cone on a plate covered with dragées and coloured sprinkles.

Move one of the loaf cakes in the middle of the round cake and cut off the overhang.

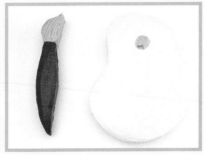

Ice (frost) the palette and brush with coloured buttercream.

Use tweezers to adorn the paintbrush with silver dragées.

at last! I am ten

1 Preheat the oven to 180°C (350°F/Gas 4). Grease the cake tins and line the bases with baking paper. Divide the cake mix evenly among the tins and bake the loaf tins for 40 minutes and the round tin for 55 minutes, or until a skewer inserted into the centre of the cakes comes out clean. Let the cakes cool in the tins for 5 minutes before turning out onto a wire rack to cool completely.

2 Level the cakes if necessary. Put the round cake on the cake board, cut in half crossways and move the pieces apart. Move one of the loaf cakes into the middle. Cut off the overhanging part of the loaf cake. Sit the other loaf cake to the left of the round cake and add the offcut to the bottom.

3 Join the cake pieces together with buttercream. Put the template of the paintbrush on the loaf cake and secure with toothpicks. Mark the line between the bristles and the handle by piercing through the paper onto the cake with a skewer or toothpick. Cut to shape.

4 Put the template of the palette on the round cake and secure with toothpicks. To make the finger hole in the palette, you can either cut through the template with a sharp knife or mark the area with a skewer and cut it out after you have removed the template.

5 Leave half the buttercream white for the palette. Put one quarter of the remaining buttercream in a bowl and tint it caramel. Put ⅓ cup of the buttercream in another bowl and tint it bright red. Leave the remaining buttercream white until needed. Spread the brown buttercream over the bristles, making furrows for texture, and spread red over the handle. Spread the palette with the white buttercream.

6 Put the chocolate melts in a heatproof bowl. Bring a saucepan of water to the boil, then remove from the heat. Sit the bowl over the pan, making sure the base of the bowl does not sit in the water. Stir occasionally until the chocolate has melted. Spoon the chocolate into a piping bag. Pipe individual hairs over the brown buttercream, leaving a narrow strip at the bottom for three rows of dragées. To finish the brush, carefully put three rows of dragées between the hairs and the handle.

7 Divide the remaining buttercream into small portions and tint different colours. Add dabs of the colours onto the palette to look like paints.

CAKE AND EQUIPMENT
22 cm (8½ inch) round tin
two 8 x 25 cm (3¼ x 10 inch) loaf (bar) tins
2 packets cake mix
30 x 30 cm (12 x 12 inch) cake board
copy of template from page 159
toothpicks or skewers

DECORATION
2 quantities buttercream from page 11
food colouring: caramel, red (we used powder for red) and other assorted colours
35 g (1¼ oz/¼ cup) chocolate melts (buttons)
silver dragées or cachous

templates

To enlarge the templates, use a photocopier to enlarge the image by the amount given. If your photocopier only enlarges to a maximum of 200%, use the measurements given in parentheses to enlarge in two steps. If you don t have access to a photocopier, draw a graph with the same size square indicated on the template, then transfer the drawing to paper.

marvin the martian

pages 18–19

100%

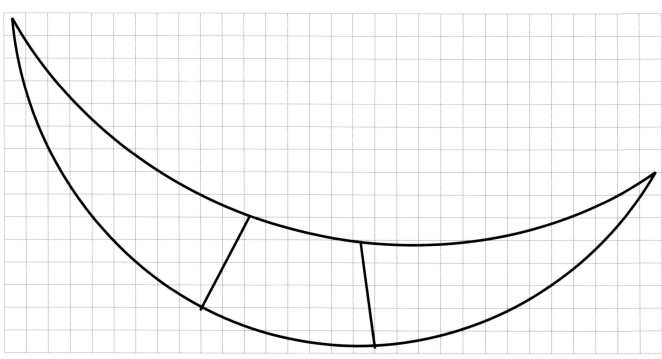

Each square = 6 mm (¹/₄ inch)

desmond the dinosaur

pages 22–23

Enlarge 260%
(200% then 130%)

Each square = 15 mm (¹/₂ inch)

splash! the mermaid

pages 24–25

Enlarge 300%
(200% then 150%)

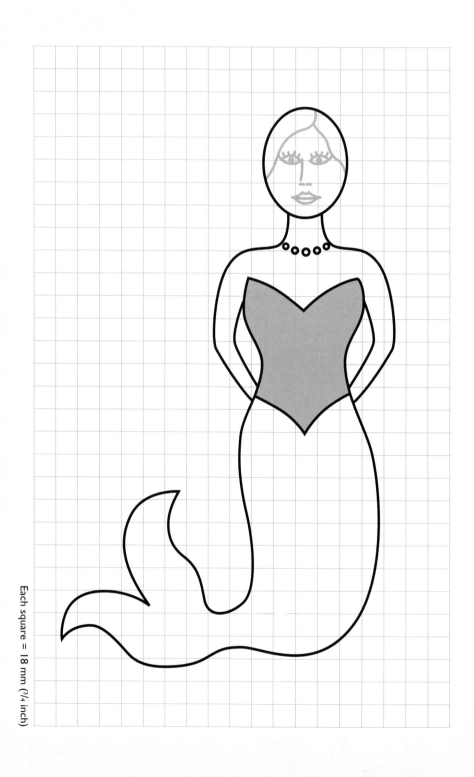

Each square = 18 mm (³/4 inch)

cranky witch

pages 26–27

Enlarge 166%
(150% then 111%)

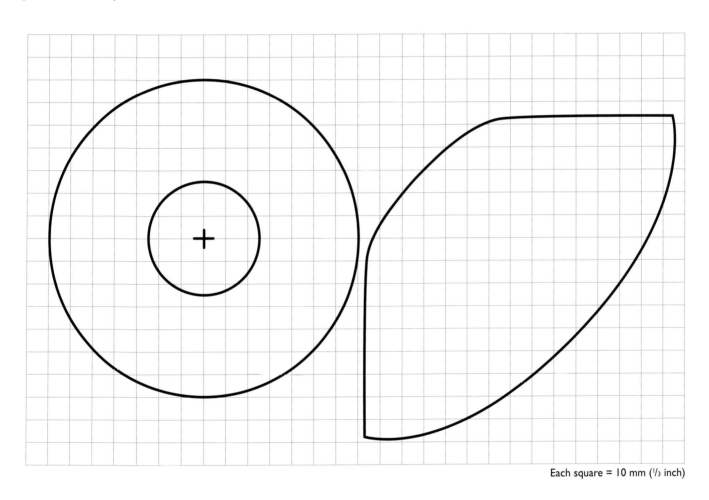

Each square = 10 mm (¹/₃ inch)

happy clown

pages 28–29

Enlarge 200%

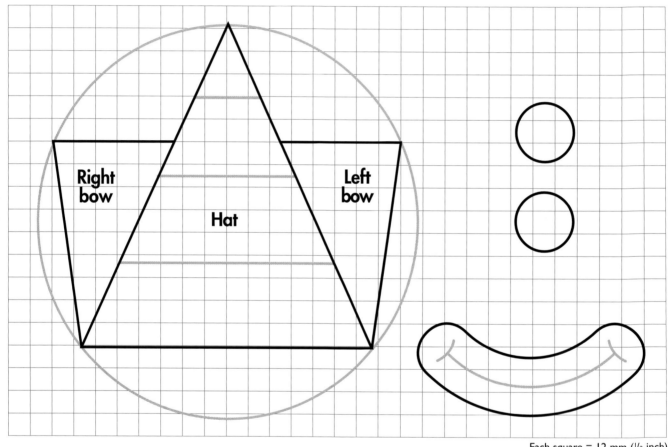

Right bow

Left bow

Hat

Each square = 12 mm (¹/₂ inch)

ferocious monster

pages 30–31

Enlarge 215%
(200% then 110%)

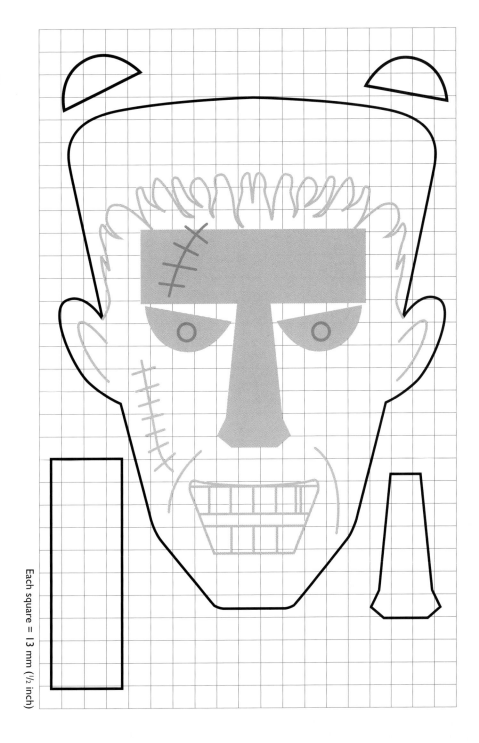

Each square = 13 mm (½ inch)

creepy-crawly caterpillar

pages 34–35

100%

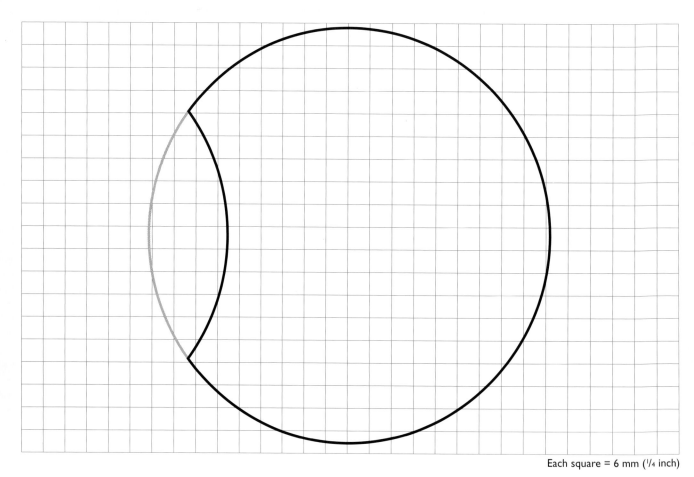

Each square = 6 mm (¹/₄ inch)

fresh as a daisy

pages 36–37

Enlarge 215%
(200% then 110%)

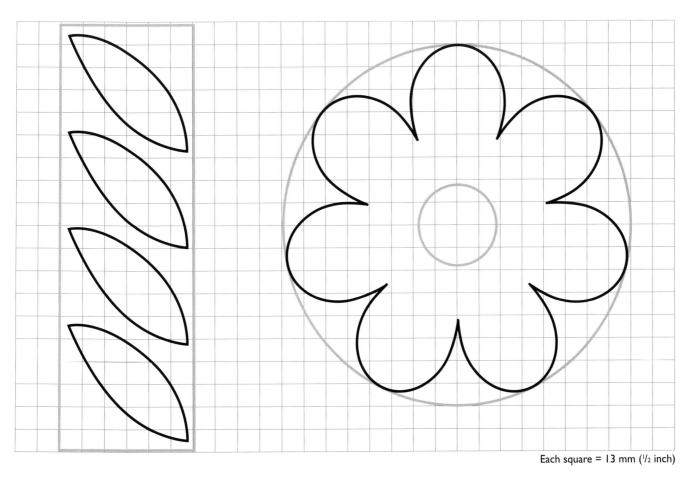

Each square = 13 mm (½ inch)

hopping rabbit

pages 38–39

Enlarge enlarge 165%

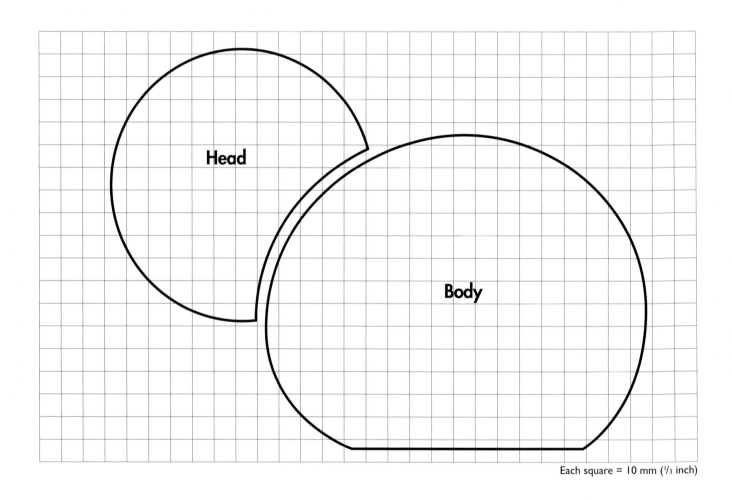

Head

Body

Each square = 10 mm (¹/₃ inch)

Enlarge 165%

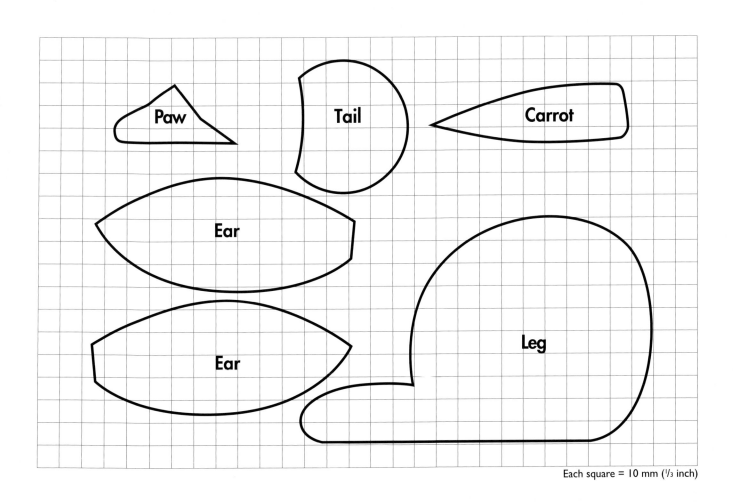

Paw

Tail

Carrot

Ear

Ear

Leg

Each square = 10 mm (¹/₃ inch)

little miss ladybird

pages 42–43

Enlarge 208%
(200% then 104%)

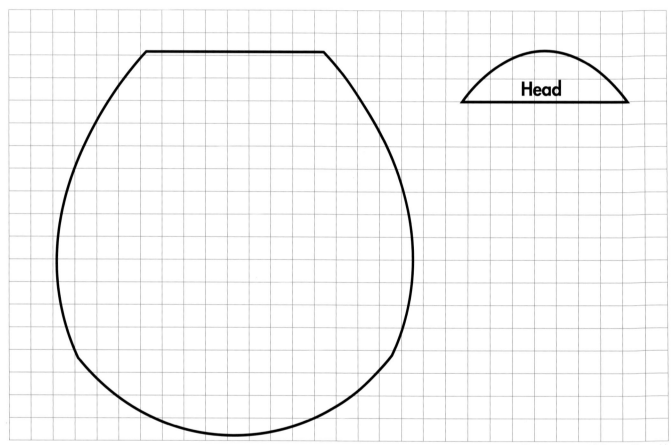

Head

Each square = 12.5 mm (¹/₂ inch)

beautiful butterfly

pages 44–45

Enlarge 165%

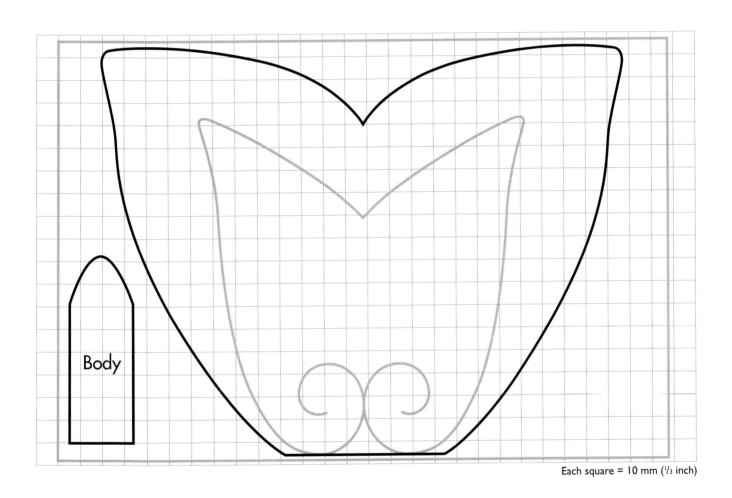

Body

Each square = 10 mm (¹/₃ inch)

tropical fish

pages 46–47

Enlarge 250%
(200% then 125%)

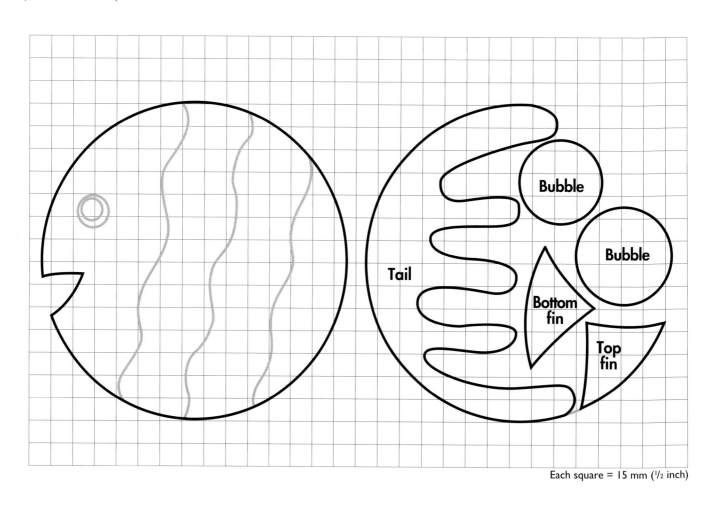

Each square = 15 mm (¹/₂ inch)

spotty the dog

pages 50–51

Enlarge 250%
(200% then 125%)

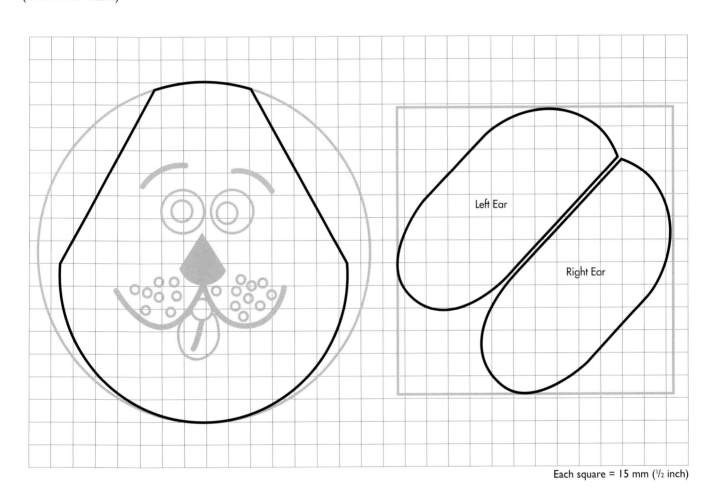

Left Ear

Right Ear

Each square = 15 mm (¹/₂ inch)

cat on a mat

pages 52–53

Enlarge 215%
(200% then 110%)

Each square = 13 mm (¹/₂ inch)

fatty the whale

pages 54–55

Enlarge 266%
(200% then 133%)

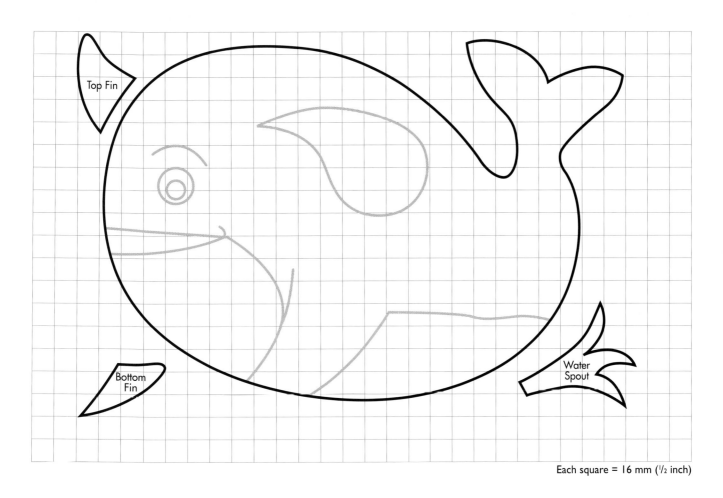

Top Fin

Bottom
Fin

Water
Spout

Each square = 16 mm (¹/₂ inch)

fighter plane

pages 62–63

Enlarge 183%

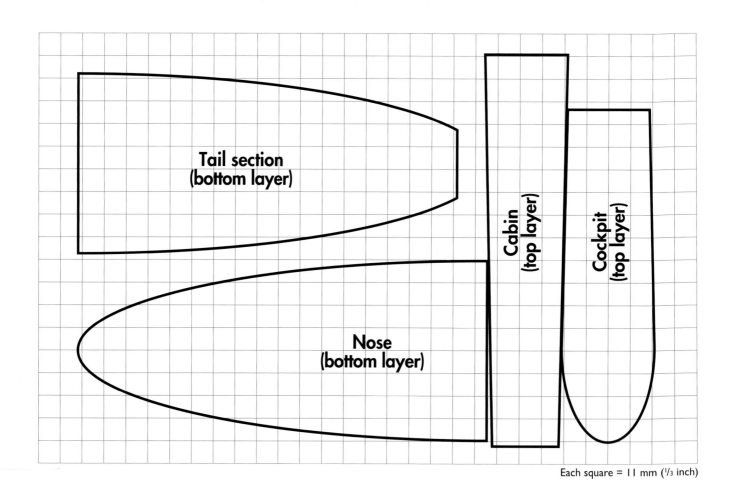

**Tail section
(bottom layer)**

**Cabin
(top layer)**

**Cockpit
(top layer)**

**Nose
(bottom layer)**

Each square = 11 mm (¹/₃ inch)

Enlarge 183%

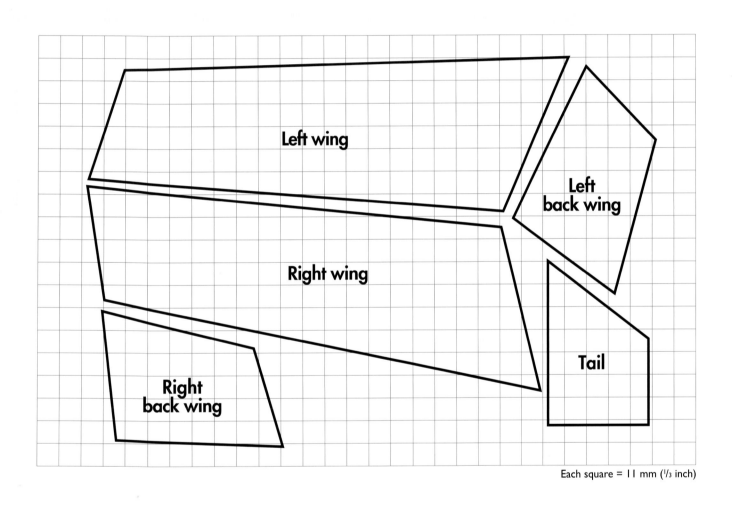

Left wing

Left
back wing

Right wing

Tail

Right
back wing

Each square = 11 mm (¹⁄₃ inch)

gnarly dude! skateboard

pages 66–67

Enlarge 165%

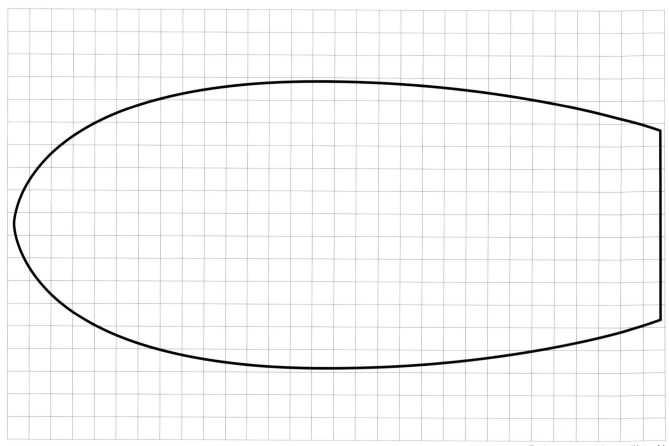

Each square = 10 mm (1/3 inch)

electric guitar

pages 68–69

Enlarge 215%
(200% then 110%)

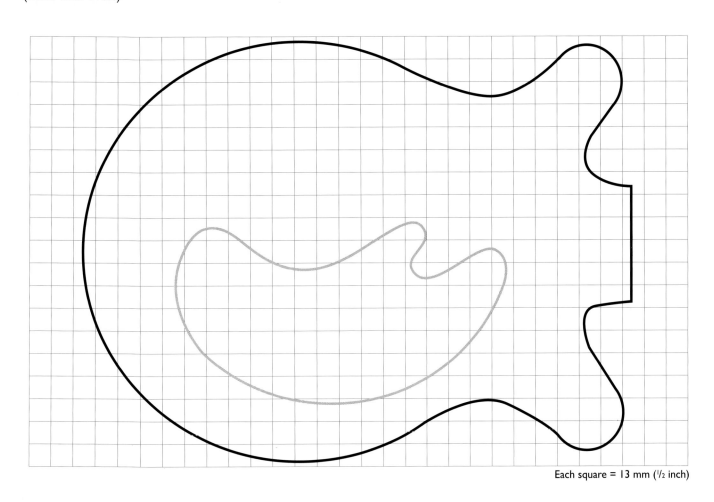

Each square = 13 mm (½ inch)

vroom vroom racing car

pages 70–71

Enlarge 200%

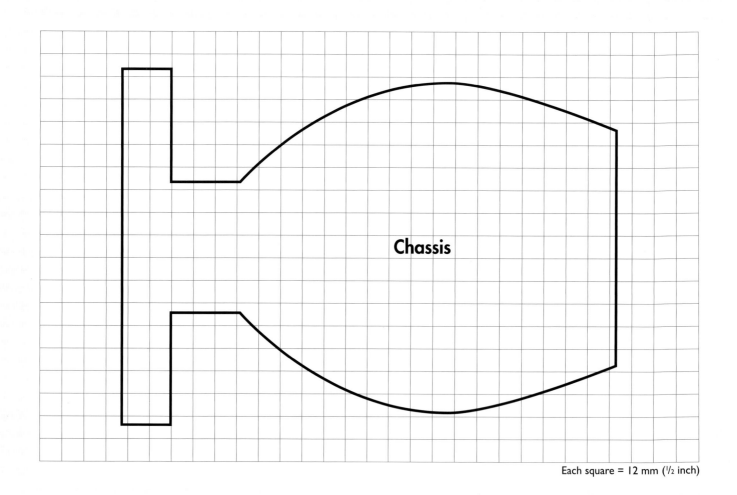

Chassis

Each square = 12 mm (¹/₂ inch)

cricket bat and ball

pages 76–77

Enlarge 150%

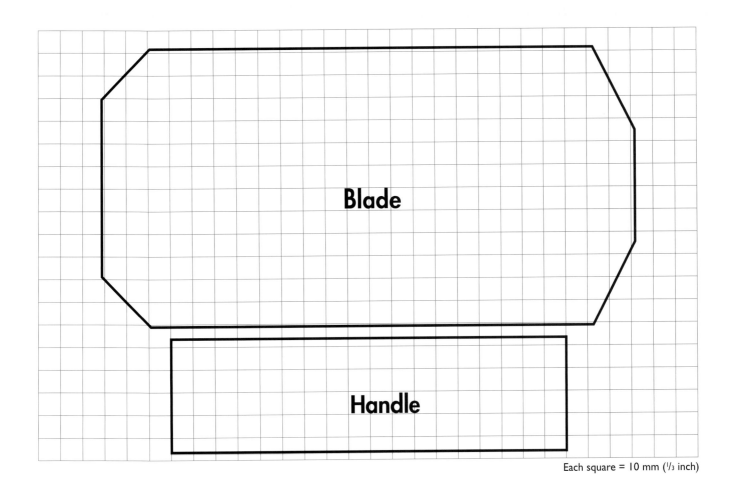

Blade

Handle

Each square = 10 mm (¹/₃ inch)

bart simpson

pages 82—83

Enlarge 266%
(200% then 133%)

Each square = 16 mm (²/₃ inch)

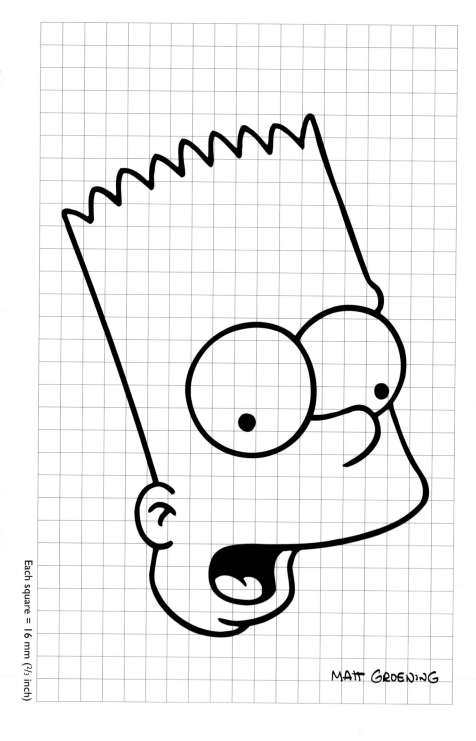

MATT GROENING

marge simpson

pages 84—85

Enlarge 333%
(200% then 167%)

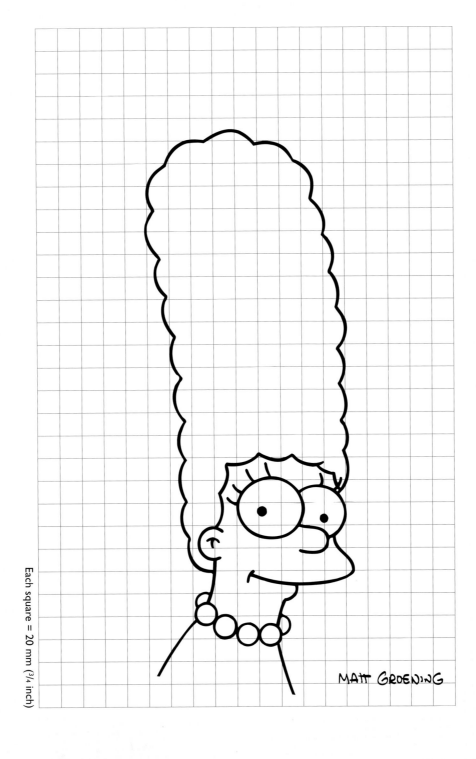

Each square = 20 mm (³/₄ inch)

MATT GROENING

homer simpson

pages 86—87

Enlarge 283%
(200% then 142%)

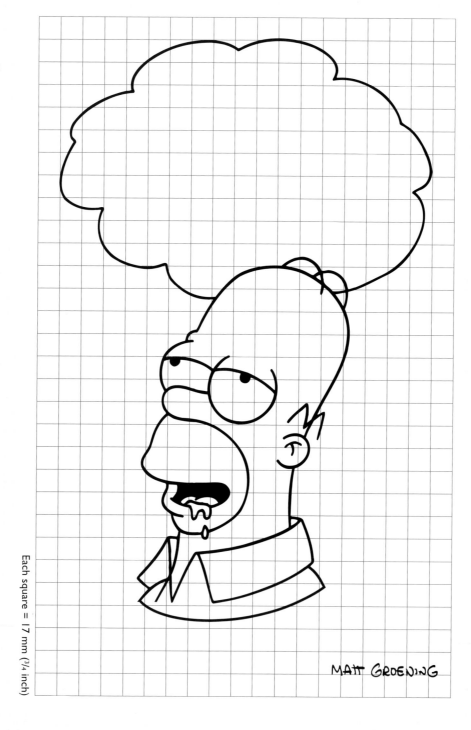

Each square = 17 mm (³/₄ inch)

MATT GROENING

lisa simpson

pages 88—89

Enlarge 283%
(200% then 142%)

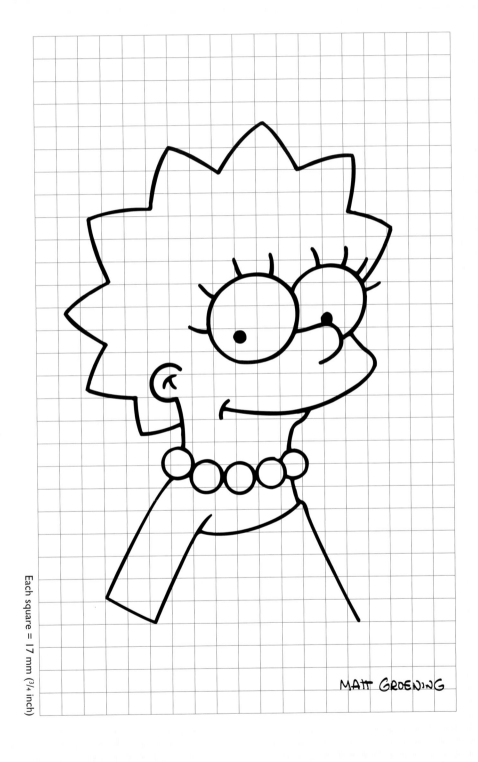

Each square = 17 mm (³/₄ inch)

MATT GROENING

maggie simpson

pages 90—91

Enlarge 283%
(200% then 142%)

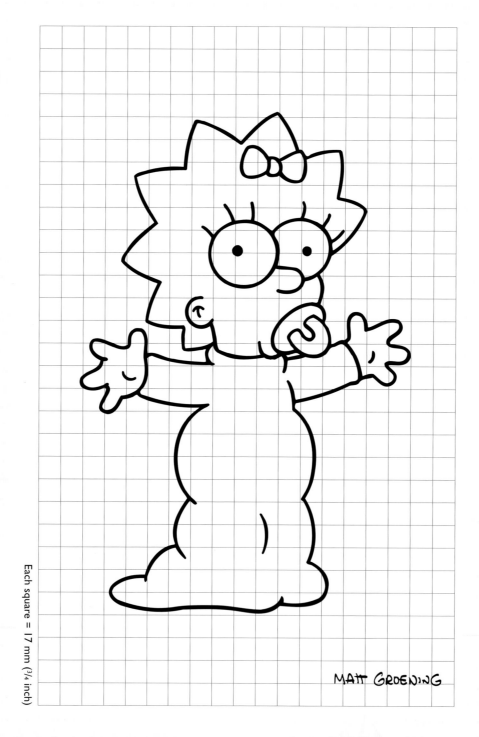

Each square = 17 mm (³/₄ inch)

MATT GROENING

santa's little helper

pages 92—93

Enlarge 283%
(200% then 142%)

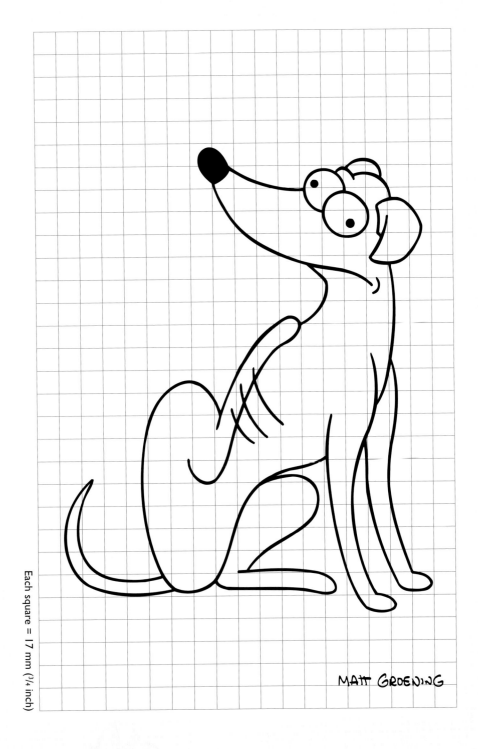

Each square = 17 mm (³/₄ inch)

MATT GROENING

mr. montgomery burns

pages 94—95

Enlarge 266%
(200% then 133%)

Each square = 17 mm (¾ inch)

MATT GROENING

head to toe bart simpson

pages 96—97

Enlarge 266%
(200% then 133%)

Each square = 16 mm (²/₃ inch)

MATT GROENING

itchy & scratchy

pages 98–99

Enlarge 300%
(200% then 150%)

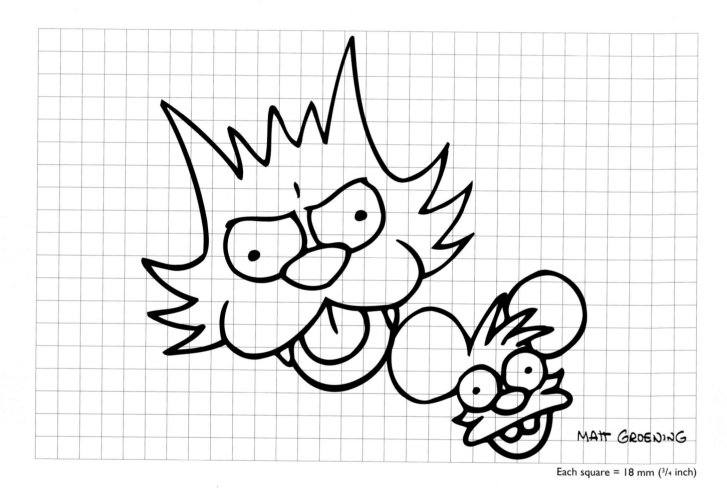

Each square = 18 mm (³/₄ inch)

krusty the clown

pages 100—101

Enlarge 350%
(200% then 175%)

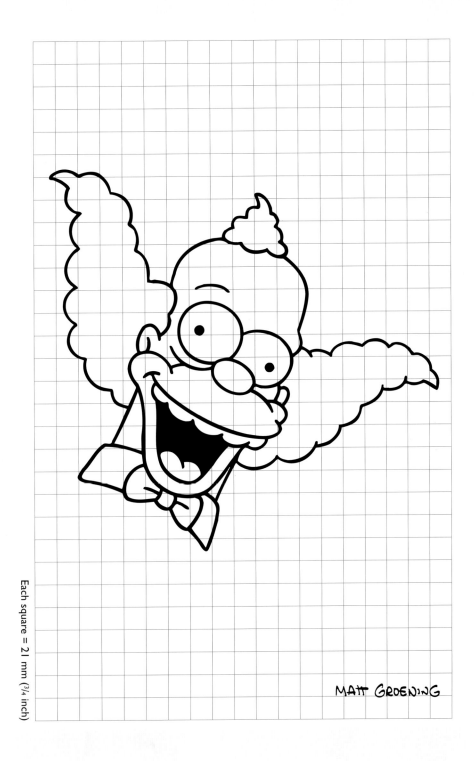

Each square = 21 mm (³/₄ inch)

MATT GROENING

snakey number two

pages 106—107

Enlarge 215%
(200% then 110%)

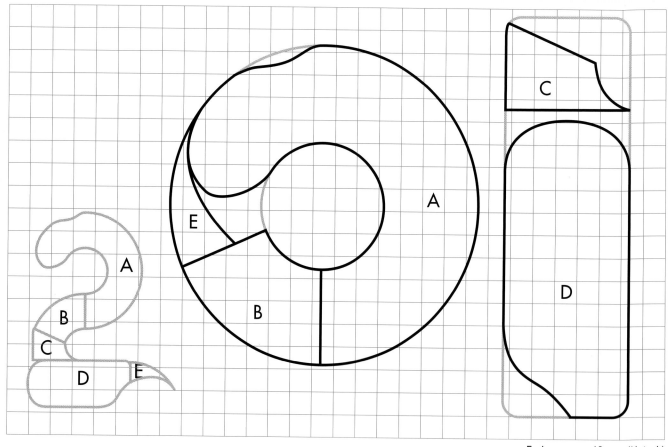

Each square = 13 mm (¹/₂ inch)

at last! I am ten

pages 122–123

Enlarge 266%
(200% then 133%)

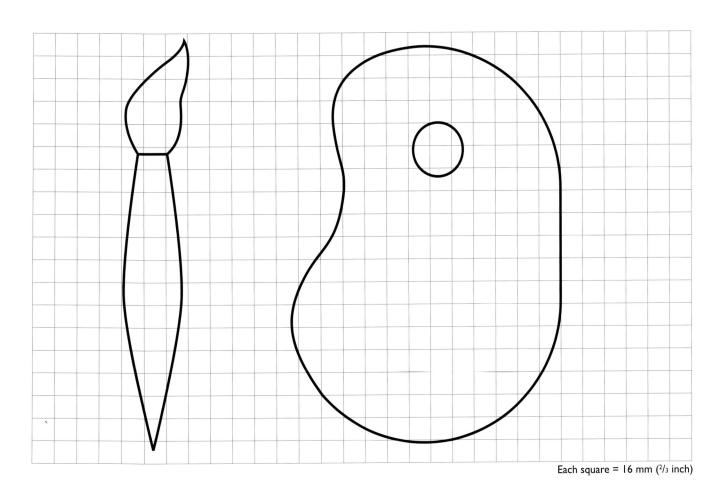

Each square = 16 mm (²/₃ inch)

index